Modern Wilderness Survival

A Practical Guide

T0062472

John Solomon

Contents

Introduction

We don't usually venture into the wilderness with the intent of staying beyond what we've planned for. But failing to prepare for such a situation – an injury, getting lost, being delayed because of weather – can turn an inconvenience into a real problem.

I started teaching survival skills in the military, where it was a student's duty to prepare for a worst-case scenario. Many of my students, who had jobs such as fighter pilots or members of special operations units, had a fairly real potential for using what I taught them. After my military service, I taught at Boy Scout campouts, Hunter Education classes, community groups, and among friends who liked to hunt and fish. I began to realize that instilling a "duty to prepare" mindset into people who spent time in the wilderness was a much harder undertaking when they didn't really believe there was the possibility they'd have to use these skills.

Never did I realize this more than when I went on hunting trip many years ago with "John." He was born and raised in Montana, and he spoke at length about his experience in the backcountry. We planned to hike several miles into a remote area for a weekend of elk hunting at his family's camp. It was a great idea, until it started.

I asked for a map of the area, and he said, "Trust me," because he didn't want to give away his family's secret spot. He carried a small daypack with a cotton sweatshirt, some rope, and book of paper matches in it – that was it. John laughed at all the gear I carried because he thought it would weigh me down. On our hike in, he lost his way and we got pounded by a rain storm. His ego kept pushing him on even though he was soaked, shivering, and dehydrated. Finally, I stopped and built a fire over his objections. He insisted he knew where he was and we squabbled about it until he was dry. He refused my offer of a rain jacket and got soaked again as we fought through thick brush in the growing darkness. I was just about to leave him to his own fate and make camp for myself when he spotted a glowing wall tent in the distance. We stumbled into camp an hour later, exhausted, and he said "You really can't get lost out here; you just keep walking until you figure out where you are." I was so frustrated with him I wanted to head back to the truck.

Over the years, I've met many other "John" characters who have a similar approach to venturing into the woods. Unfortunately, most don't really want to change the way they do things. Just by reading this far into it, though, I know that *you* have not only an interest in being safe in the wilderness, but also a desire to learn how. My hope is to give you simple, effective tips that you can use the minute you put this book down, and be able to remember for many years to come.

Learning survival skills is really quite simple. You don't need to know how to live for months as a primitive dweller making buckskins and chipping spear points in order to survive in the woods. These skills are great to know and obviously can be of tremendous help. But, they also take a long time to master, and cannot be learned simply by reading a book. In contrast, this book will focus on 1) being prepared, which means carrying survival tools into the wilderness to begin with, and 2) being able to survive and sustain for at least three days, which is the average duration of most survival situations you might encounter. And frankly, if you are prepared to make it three days, you will be able to make it for several more. There are many reasons you might get stuck, but an important adjustment to make right now is to realize: *It is not a bad thing to spend an unexpected night in the woods*. I've even had a few nights out that were downright fun! Call it extreme camping, unplanned adventure, whatever – just don't fear it. I'll give you an example:

I was climbing around some rocky cliffs in southeastern Idaho with my best friend one fall day. We found ourselves stuck in the dark as we tried to pick through a steep canyon and get back to camp. On top of that, it was getting cold and the wind started blowing pretty hard. The safest thing to do was avoid the treacherous cliffs in the dark and camp overnight where we were – we could resume our descent in the morning. My buddy hadn't spent an unplanned night out before and he wasn't so sure about the idea. An hour later, we relaxed in a warm, secure shelter by a fire and stayed comfortable while the wind howled and the temperature dropped. We resumed our climb down when it got light and made it back to camp just fine. My buddy gained a lot of confidence in his abilities and now prepares for these unexpected circumstances a little differently.

I hope you will see it differently, too, but you are in an advantageous position. You can gain this perspective, and the skills you need, without having to face a dire situation. This book focuses on giving you easy to learn and easy to use techniques that will get you through a survival situation. These are the building blocks of being safe in the wilderness. You are already taking the first and most critical step: preparation. So let's get started.

Chapter 1 – Preparation

Let's start with a hypothetical example: Say you are walking home one night and get attacked in an alley by three thugs. Your body and mind will be flooded with the "fight or flight" surge, and you will have to spring into action immediately. You will be feeling fear and anger at the same time you are trying to make decisions. It's scary. And depending on your split-second reactions, the outcome can go either way in a hurry. Now let's step back. If you are well trained in fighting, and had confidence in your abilities, would you feel different? Would the outcome change? Take it back one more step. What if you realized that walking down that alley at night might not be the best idea, and you stayed on the lighted sidewalks instead? By doing so, you've avoided the attack altogether, and that's the most positive outcome possible.

That's really the idea of preparing for wilderness survival. You want to do as much as possible before you get to the wilderness to eliminate the situations where we have to switch to survival mode. But, if you are faced with a survival situation, you will be prepared, which will help you deal with the challenge much more rationally, and with minimal fear.

Preparation is the cornerstone of survival skills – its importance cannot be overemphasized. That means having the right tools for surviving in the woods, having a complete picture of where you are going, knowing what to expect from the weather, being aware of how to avoid problems, and making sure there are people who can help if you get stuck. Unfortunately, preparation is probably the most overlooked aspect of learning survival skills. So let's make it easy by breaking it down into four steps.

STEP 1 – EQUIPMENT

Obviously, we must have adequate tools with us in the wilderness to meet our needs in unexpected situations. Everyone has unique factors that determine what they carry, such as size, weight, and budget. Several companies have taken the guesswork out of putting together a survival kit by offering pre-assembled kits. The options are wide in both what they have to offer and how much they cost (See Chapter 15 for a few places to start). But no matter what, you need to address "the basics" listed below, which will get you through just about any situation you find yourself in.

Knife

The key words to remember with this tool are *sharp* and *sturdy*. Several compact multi-tool knives are available, and having extra tools can be helpful. But sometimes having more gadgets means having less knife. Avoid the gimmicky "50-in-1" tools and go for something simple. Knives equipped with an extra saw-tooth blade are a handy way to increase your abilities. New technologies in material and construction have also brought about featherweight knives that are great tools.

A SHARP, STURDY KNIFE IS AN IMPORTANT SURVIVAL TOOL. THE SAW BLADE ADDS VERSATILITY.

Firemaking Tools

Be sure you can easily start three fires with what you carry in your kit. Never carry "just enough" for one. There are many unforeseen circumstances that can ruin your first attempt, and having more than one backup is safest. Pack a couple dozen wooden strike-anywhere matches (avoid paper matches) and dip them in paraffin, wrap in plastic, or secure in a waterproof match case. Pack at least one back-up ignition source. There are a few storm-proof lighters on the market that work quite well, justifying the extra expense. They usually incorporate some sort of rubber gaskets to protect the ignition source and light up like a small torch. A regular butane lighter will work well too. I also carry a "metal match," which is a magnesium-based striker similar to flints in a lighter, but bigger. They provide thousands of white-hot strikes and last many seasons. Include tinder in your kit to ensure you can get a sustainable flame established for igniting kindling (see Chapter 5 for more on tinder). Try out the fire-starting tools you have, especially if you just bought them or have never used similar items before. You may realize you don't like them or they don't work as well as advertised. Better to learn this now than on a cold, rainy night when your life depends on it.

Shelter Material

A military-style poncho is hard to beat for durability, but an 8' X 10' or 9 'x 12' piece of 2-mil painter's plastic is lighter and just as versatile (and typically much less expensive). One of my favorite pieces of gear is a double-sided lightweight nylon tarp. It is red on one side and silver on the other – it can be both a shelter and a signal at the same time. It has grommets in the corner and reinforced edges. My best friend and I made a lean-to out of one in high wind and it held up well through the night. It's not as strong as a military poncho, but lighter and generally less expensive. I would recommend avoiding the small foil-type "space blankets" that are available in most sporting goods stores. In my opinion, they are not durable, are difficult to keep in place, and minimally effective. Compact "emergency sleeping bags" are a better option. They are typically made from the same sort of reflective space-blanket material, but are thicker and more durable. They are built in a long tube shape, sort of like a big garbage bag, and are designed to trap body heat.

A SIMPLE SHELTER CONSTRUCTED USING 2-MIL PLASTIC

Flashlight

Survival tool? If you have to spend a night in the woods, a reliable mini-flashlight or headlamp in your kit can help you find what you need to survive without falling off a cliff or poking an eye out. Keychain-sized LED lights are compact and helpful in a pinch, but lack brightness and durability. There are LED-headlamps that weigh a few ounces and cost less than $20, and headbands that will let you make a $10 AA flashlight into a hands-free device. Don't forget extra batteries and bulbs.

A HANDS-FREE LIGHT SOURCE IS VALUABLE IN SURVIVAL SITUATIONS

Rope

Fifty feet should be enough to tie up a shelter and fashion a drying rack for your clothes, with plenty to spare. Military parachute cord is great for survival kits – it's strong and the core is composed of smaller nylon strands that can be used for sewing, fishing, and a host of other needs. Most hardware stores and some sporting goods stores sell different sizes of nylon cord by the foot. A bundle of 1/8" cord is lightweight and won't hurt your wallet, but will work perfectly in the woods.

Compass

This should be in addition to whatever compass or global positioning satellite (GPS) unit you use for navigation – it's a "just-in-case" item. Chapter 2 will discuss particulars on how to use a compass, as well as different types available on the market.

Signals

A whistle and a signaling mirror are minimums. Both can be found in lightweight plastic models that are nearly indestructible and inexpensive. Flares are also effective in certain situations, but price and weight can be limiting.

Water Collection

It is wise to start your journey with a supply of drinking water at hand (I try to keep 2 quarts with me all the time). It's heavy, but worth it on extended hikes. In a situation where you don't have water bottles, a one-gallon zip-lock freezer bag is excellent for gathering and storing. It weighs almost nothing and can fold up into a tiny bundle. A length of flexible rubber tubing (also available by the foot in host hardware stores, sometimes referred to as "surgical tubing") will enable you to suck water from seep springs or rain puddles in hard to reach spots. A metal cup is always a great tool here, as you can melt snow, boil water for purification, and cook with it. Last, a method of purification is critical. A variety of tablets and drops are available, as well as some pocket-sized filter devices.

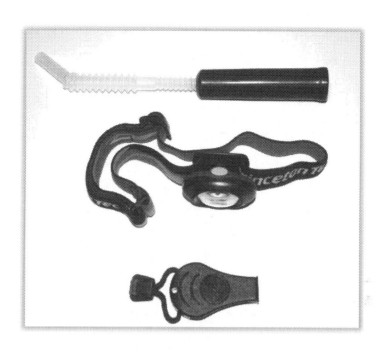

THREE ITEMS I ALWAYS KEEP IN MY KIT:
STRAW-STYLE WATER FILTER (TOP)
LED HEADLAMP (MIDDLE)
WHISTLE (BOTTOM)

Food

Carrying an energy bar or two can help get you through a night in the woods more comfortably; they're small and loaded with carbohydrates. These should not be included as snacks or meals, but are set aside specifically for emergency situations. Packing some fishing line and a few hooks, and a length of snare wire, can also help supplement your diet if you are stuck.

First Aid

Personally, I pack basic first aid items in my survival kit. If I am venturing into a remote backcountry area, I will carry a supplemental first aid kit as well, which has an extensive list of items. The basics, however, should address common injuries you might encounter, such as cuts, splinters, blisters, and burns. Of course, there are many variations of each, and this part of your survival kit is open to personal interpretation. Specifically, you need to include any personal medications (including an extra set of glasses if you wear them), which will be necessary for health if you are stuck for several days. Periodically update these medications as they could expire. Samples of other basic items to include are band-aids, alcohol wipes, antibiotic ointment, tweezers, moleskin, gauze pad(s), and a small roll of medical tape. Additional items could include a soft splint, ACE wraps, triangular bandage, and safety pins.

Environmental Considerations

You also need to remember the particular challenges of the environment you are going into. If you will be spending time in snowy conditions, consider carrying a metal cup for melting snow. If it is a rain forest, a hatchet will help tremendously with shelter construction and utilizing dry wood sources. In a desert environment, a wide-brimmed hat, sunglasses, and a small tarp for shade are the bare minimum.

Carry Methods

Next, decide how you are going to carry all this stuff. A kit that is bulky or heavy will get left behind, and that violates the cardinal rule – ALWAYS have your survival kit with you. Some folks like to have one "do-all" kit that they carry with them regardless of where they are, and some like to add or take away certain items as circumstances dictate (e.g., weight, environment, etc.). This is a personal choice. I do both: one kit with all the basics goes everywhere, and I add items to my pack that are particular for the trip. You also need to protect your survival tools from the environment – that means waterproof. Keep them organized – be sure to know what you have and where to find it. Desperately searching for your matches on a cold, dark night can lead to panic.

🍁 A waterproof drawstring bag can be created with little effort by sewing together pieces of old nylon ponchos – toss the bundle in any pack and know you've got everything you need to get through an emergency. You can also buy nylon drawstring bags in most sporting goods stores for a few dollars.

🍁 Generally, belt pouches are big enough to fit all the basics but small enough to be unobtrusive. Plus, you can put it in your pack while hiking but slide it on your belt for a quick peek over the next hill when you get to camp.

🍁 A two-piece snap-together soap dish works great as a kit container because it is waterproof and durable, and the size is ideal. Plus they only cost a dollar or two – find them in the grocery store's "Travel Items" section.

🌑 A one-gallon heavy-duty freezer bag is great for keeping items together, and as you know, it can pull double duty for collecting and storing water.

🌑 Some people use horses, mountain bikes, or all-terrain vehicles (ATVs) in the outdoors and carry their gear in saddlebags where weight really isn't a limiting factor. This is great if you will always be with your vehicle or pack animal. Consider having a small kit that can go with you as well in case you separate from your means of transportation.

🌑 I know a few people who carry a day pack or fanny pack full of survival equipment. This is fine, and it lets you carry all kinds of equipment. However, if it is heavy or cumbersome, it will get left behind, especially on short walks, when it might be considered "too much."

A VARIETY OF OPTIONS FOR CARRYING SURVIVAL
EQUIPMENT

STEP 2 – CLOTHING

Nowhere is preparation more apparent than in the clothing you wear into the woods. The right clothing protects you from the elements by keeping you dry and comfortable. The wrong clothing can be uncomfortable at best, and can actually rob your body of heat. It is important to wear clothing that is suited for the conditions now, but also to be prepared for conditions that may arise later (like the saying goes in the mountains, if you don't like the weather, just wait an hour – it will change).

The most efficient way to account for several eventualities is to dress in layers. This allows you to adjust your body heat quickly and easily. Think of your layers as a 3-part system.

Layer 1 – Next to Your Skin

Sweat reduces the thermal efficiency of your clothing from the inside out by first eliminating (filling) dead air space in clothing fibers. The moisture then creates heat loss by conducting heat away from your skin. The most problematic material in this regard is cotton, known for its absorbency. A cotton shirt will quickly soak with sweat and cling to your body like a wet glove, and it's notoriously slow to dry. In cooler conditions this is a recipe for hypothermia, but in hot climates, the goal is different: you want to allow sweat to cool your body by evaporating off your skin and clothing. Obviously lightweight cotton clothing can work pretty well in such circumstances, but beware: getting caught with damp, clammy clothes on when the sun goes down is an invitation for problems, even in mild conditions.

An alternative to cotton is synthetic micro-fleece. It has a soft, suede-like feel and carries about the same bulk as a cotton shirt.

However, the synthetic fibers wick the moisture away from your skin and do not absorb or trap it in the garment. Conversely, the small layer of air in the material provides enough protection to prevent shivering when the sun goes behind the clouds. Another option is to wear polypropylene undergarments. They also wick moisture away from your skin and dry quickly if damp. You can find polypropylene in lightweight, form-fitting styles as well as heavyweight fleeced versions. They retain insulating properties when wet and don't weigh you down as much as wool does.

Layer 2 – Insulating

In cold weather, additional layers of insulating clothing are usually necessary to keep you warm. Goose down is effective for this requirement because it gets fantastic loft and traps air well, but it is beefy and becomes ineffective if wet. You can also consider a couple layers of fleece or light wool. The layers will allow you to micro-adjust on the go: strip down while you're hiking, and add them on when you stop to rest or the weather turns cold. As an added benefit, both wool and fleece retain a good percentage of thermal efficiency if they get wet.

Don't forget headgear, and don't rely on a ball cap if it's cold. There are some great products that are built like removable hoods that can be worn in a variety of configurations to meet changing needs, and they add the bonus of covering your neck. Remember to take your hat off during strenuous hikes. Your head produces a lot of heat, and regulating temperature this way will help reduce sweating. Feet should also get consideration, and insulating principles (such as layering polypropylene and wool) work the same way inside your boots. Make sure laces aren't so tight they inhibit good circulation.

Layer 3 – Outer Shell

Lastly, you need to protect your body and the warmth you've created around it. The key is to keep wind and precipitation on the outside, but allow moisture created by your body to escape. Common rubberized nylon rain suits are economical but they really don't breathe. Gore-tex and Wind stopper fabrics are excellent barriers and yet still porous enough to allow water vapor from perspiration to escape. And they tend to have a heavier price tag.

Hand coverings fall in this category, too. Mittens keep your fingers together, allowing them to share heat. Gloves isolate fingers and make each one rely on circulation for warmth, but they do have better dexterity. Some mittens have fold-back finger portions so you can have the best of both worlds. I like military surplus wool glove liners, one or two layers depending on the conditions. A few companies are making Gore-tex backed fleece gloves, and even though the price can be hefty, they are worth it in nasty conditions.

Improvising

* If you're caught out for a night with inadequate insulating clothing, you can create dead air space for warmth by stuffing dry leaves or dead grass between the layers of the clothing you are wearing. You might look funny, but you'll be warm.

❧ You can find compact plastic ponchos at many sporting goods stores, and they typically cost a couple of dollars. They are handy emergency moisture barriers that easily fit in a pocket. If you don't want to spend the money, use a heavyweight garbage bag instead. Tear holes in the corners for your arms, and poke a hole in the middle of the bottom seam for your head. It's not very durable, but it can shed water and trap heat in a pinch.

❧ A fleece or wool vest and stocking hat can really help if you are stuck out for a night. The stocking hat traps heat in an area that radiates up to 50% of your body heat and the vest is a cocoon for vital organs – both will help you sleep warmer and maintain a comfortable body temperature.

STEP 3 - PRE-TRIP RESEARCH

Now that your gear and clothing are selected, you'll need to equip your mind. You might be preparing for a trip months in advance, or it could be a quick decision to overnight somewhere for the weekend. Either way, you still need to gather as much information as possible before you go.

Weather

The Internet is a great research tool, and www.weather.com is a good place to find not only current conditions, but also a 10-day forecast, as well as average temperature and precipitation for every day of the year in a selected region. Pay attention to projected snow lines (the elevation at which rain will turn to snow) if you are traveling to the high country. I've camped in two feet of snow in June, so it is never out of season at the mountaintops.

Maps

Use topographic maps when hiking and planning because they accurately depict the terrain. They use contour lines to illustrate terrain features and indicate elevation. Maps with a scale of 1:24,000 provide excellent detail but will not cover a large piece of ground. A 1:50,000 scale usually finds a happy medium between detail and area. Check the date of the map when you buy it, Roads, clear-cuts, and buildings are time-sensitive features. Protect your map from the environment by laminating it, sealing it in a plastic baggie, or carrying it in a waterproof case (there are several styles that can easily fit in a cargo pocket). National Geographic has developed a touch-screen kiosk that prints seamless topographic maps on waterproof paper. You can pick the area to be mapped, the scale, and the dimensions of the map you want (see Chapter 15 for additional sources). Last, don't cut out a small section of a map to use for reference. It may save a little room in your pocket, but if you happen to wander outside the small square you cut out, or need to look at distant terrain features for reference when you are disoriented, you're out of luck.

Work the Phone

A few last-minute phone calls to the closest US Forest Service Ranger Station will often give you current information about the quality of the trail where you are heading and any problems you might encounter. For high country trips, this can be especially helpful for predicting the possibility of snow and slide areas. Plus, you can talk over your planned trek with the rangers and let them know what you are planning to do. Additionally, some areas, especially national parks, will require you to check in or obtain a permit before you enter certain wilderness areas.

STEP 4 – ITINERARY

Your last step before heading out the door on a trip is to provide a written itinerary to a friend or loved one whom you trust. This itinerary should include your travel route(s), camp site(s), a vehicle description and license plate number, medical conditions, names of everyone in your party, your cell phone number (if you carry one), and a no-later-than return time. I usually write all this information in the margin area of a map showing where I'll be with routes and camps highlighted. If available, I include phone numbers for the closest search and rescue contact as well as the county sheriff's office. These steps will save valuable time if you are delayed, lost, or hurt, and you don't want a distressed friend or loved one to be frantically trying to decide whom to call if you aren't home when you said you would be.

If you decide to change your itinerary in mid-stream, let someone know and leave a note in your vehicle. That vehicle will usually be the starting point for a search and can yield valuable clues to your whereabouts. It is also wise to leave a copy of your itinerary with the closest ranger station, even if not required, for safety and peace of mind.

Out-the-door Checklist

- ○ Survival kit

- ○ Clothing for now and later

- ○ Map(s)

- ○ Check the weather

- ○ Check trail conditions (if necessary)

- ○ Fill-out detailed itinerary and leave it with someone you trust

    - ○ Vehicle description and license plate

    - ○ Where you will be and when you will return

    - ○ Who to call if you don't return

Chapter 2 – Staying Found

Many survival situations can be averted by knowing where you are and (more important) where you are going – in other words, not getting lost. Some people might imagine getting lost in the wilderness as an outback adventure gone wrong. That certainly is one scenario, but people can also get turned around in areas they are intimately familiar with. As an example, I started hunting in the wide-open spaces of southeastern Idaho and the mountains of Montana – BIG country – and I didn't seem to have much trouble navigating around. But when I hunted on our farm in Pennsylvania, a 600-acre parcel of dense hardwoods, I walked in circles and was constantly getting mixed up on my routes. There were roads and houses close by, but once in the woods, everything looked the same! Nothing is off limits for getting lost, and here are a few basic principles that will help you avoid it.

Constant Awareness

I freely admit that I'm easily distracted in the woods. It doesn't take much – a chipmunk, some interesting flowers, a rabbit – and I'm off on a diversion from whatever I was planning to do. This can be fun, but it can also lead to episodes of "Where am I?" and "How the heck did I get *here*?" This is all the more reason to keep an eye on major landmarks, the terrain, and remaining daylight.

First, pick out a few large, easily distinguishable landmarks and maintain an idea of what direction you are (or should be) from them. This might not be possible in some areas, such as the farm I described before. In a situation such as that, I like to look over my map before setting out and survey the area as much as possible, describing to myself what my route should look like, feel like, and even sound like in some instances. It never hurts to have a detailed mental picture. Knowing the layout around you (a major road to the south, a river to the east, etc.) is important even if you can't see it immediately. If you get turned around and stumble into one of them, you can get reoriented to where you are a lot quicker.

Your other senses will help, as well, such as hearing a creek you know should be on your right, or noticing that you are starting to walk downhill when you should be in a flat area. The terrain can tell you a lot if you pay attention.

Last, be aware of the daylight remaining. Why is this important when you are trying to

navigate? It's part of being constantly aware of
your situation and surroundings, which will help
you make better decisions. If you have five miles
to go through rough terrain and the sun is sitting
on the horizon, it's time to make preparations for a
night in the woods (unless you know exactly how to
get to your destination). Also, being conscious of
the time (i.e., remaining daylight) should tell you
when it's time to turn around if you are doing an
out-and-back trip so you are back by dark. Don't
get me wrong, there's nothing that says you can't
hike at night. If you are prepared to do so and
know where you are going, go for it. Otherwise,
factor daylight into your plans.

USE LANDMARKS AND CONSULT YOUR MAP FREQUENTLY

Cardinal Directions

Keeping track of the four directions (north, south, east, and west) is critical if you are going to make sense of where you are and where you need to go. I carry a button compass on a lanyard around my neck or in a pocket all the time when I hike. This is what ultimately saved me on the farm and kept me from walking in circles.

Stick and Shadow

If you don't have a compass, you can still figure out the cardinal directions. Here's the simplest way I've found that is easy to remember and even easier to do.

1. Find a flat spot of ground and clear it down to soil (or, if you are in snow, just find a flat, smooth spot).

2. Push a stick into the ground (length isn't critical, but something around 18" and slender seems to work best for me).

3. Note where the shadow of the stick is on the ground and mark the end of the shadow (the "top" of the stick as is projected on the ground) with a rock.

4. Wait 15 minutes and repeat. Do this three or four times, and you will see a line of rocks. This line will be an east-west running line. If you bisect the east-west line at a 90-degree angle, you will have a north-south running line.

Navigation

The basic techniques for using a map and compass are not complicated, but the first rule you MUST learn is to *trust them*. Don't try to convince yourself that the compass doesn't know which way north really is, or that your map is wrong because you can't find the mountain you thought you were on. And if you rely solely on the compass, or conversely, the map, you will only get 50% of the information available to prevent you from getting off track. Don't settle for half the story. Use them both.

Maps

🦡 Topographic maps most accurately depict the terrain – they use contour lines to draw features and show changes in elevation.

❧ Scale is depicted as a ratio, such as 1:24,000. This simply means that one unit on the map is equal to 24,000 units on the ground. The larger the ratio, the less detail you will be able to see with the contour lines.

❧ North on a map is usually at the top. Magnetic north is the direction your compass points due to magnetic fields that cover the earth. The two can be slightly different depending on where you are on the globe. In the lower margin of your map you will find a magnetic declination scale, which will tell you what the difference between the two is. If you are going to plot routes using a compass, you need to make sure you orient the map to magnetic north, so the map and compass agree on what north really is.

❧ Check the date of the map when you buy it – roads, clear-cuts, and buildings are time-sensitive features.

❧ Keep your map handy and refer to it often. It's a confidence booster and you'll gain familiarity with the area quickly.

❧ If you spend a lot of time walking in the woods, count the number of paces it takes you to cover a known distance. A pace is every time the same foot hits the ground (for example, count each time you step with your left). Get yourself a known pace count for ¼ mile or a kilometer or some other fixed distance you refer to often (the running track at a local high school is a great way to get this done one evening). Keep in mind that pace count will go up significantly in steep terrain. You can use this general figure to track your progress on your line of travel, and it will help you narrow down the area you're in so you can pick out landmarks. This added information helps you maintain a more accurate location on your map.

Compasses

There are several compass designs on the market today. The most basic is a button compass that you can pin onto your clothes, hang around your neck on a cord, or keep tucked in a pocket. They are good for maintaining your cardinal directions and keeping you on course. A second style is the base plate compass, best suited for plotting routes on a map. It is generally constructed of clear plastic and has measurement markings on it to use in conjunction with the map. There are also orienteering compasses, military lensatic compasses, and even digital compasses. They will all get the job done, but you don't need anything fancy or expensive to get around in the woods.

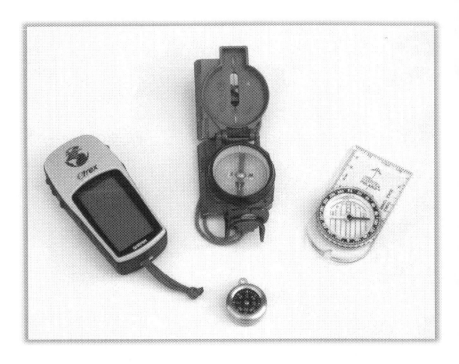

CLOCKWISE FROM TOP: MILITARY-STYLE LENSATIC COMPASS, BASE PLATE COMPASS (SILVA), BUTTON COMPASS (MARBLE'S), GPS (GARMIN eTREX)

Compasses use a magnetized needle to tell you which way north is. Because it is magnetized, the needle is sensitive to metal.

Keep it away from your body and metal objects when you are trying to get a heading, and keep the compass level as most use a rotating needle that needs to move freely. The best way to accomplish all this is to stand still, holding the compass level and out in front of your body. Give the compass a few seconds to adjust and take a reading and do it again to double check.

PHOTO BY HEATHER SOLOMON

Here's how to use a compass for simple point-to-point navigation when you can see your objective from a distance:

1. Stand with your compass as described above

2. Rotate your body and face the target (mountain peak, camp, vehicle – whatever you need to navigate to)

3. Keeping the compass in front of your body (between you and the target), read the number or symbol on the side of the compass closest to the target

4. Double check it; this is your heading

When you start to navigate, stop periodically and check your compass. Go through steps #1 - #4 above and walk on your heading. In some places, it might be possible to keep the target in sight, and that will help. But if you get into a canyon, or walk through thick timber, stop more often to check your compass. This will help you keep a straighter line of travel.

The human instinct is to take the path of least resistance. If you are navigating along the slope of a ridge or hillside, your tendency will be to "slide" a heading down hill, meaning you will be moving forward and laterally downhill at the same time. An effective way to counter this is to pick a distinguishable object as far ahead on your heading as you can see, then put your compass away and hike straight to it, rather than stopping often and re-shooting a heading. This helps prevent the "slide" and lets you better pick your path around difficult terrain or obstacles. When you get to the object you picked, step around it to one side and take another bearing – then pick another object up ahead. When you get to the next one, step around to the opposite side as the one before. If you consistently step to one side, you can move off your original line of travel by several meters over a one or two kilometer trek, and that's enough to miss a pinpoint destination.

There are many other ways to use a compass for navigating. However, using the technique I outlined above has worked in many situations for me, and I'm sure it will help you (See Chapter 14 for additional reading).

Global Positioning Satellite (GPS)

A GPS unit is a hand-held electronic device that utilizes signals from numerous satellites orbiting the earth to triangulate your position. A

GPS runs on batteries and works best when you have open sky above you. Some people are intimidated by having to learn how to use one, and I'll admit it took me a while to finally buy one. But when I did, I sat down and read the instruction manual (many of which are pretty easy to understand), and I practiced with it in my back yard. The reason I say this is many folks toss a GPS in their pack and expect that it will tell them how to get home if they just turn it on. Wrong. It takes effort on your part, starting with knowing how to use it. I cannot overemphasize that point. Once you understand the basic functions of your unit, and how the buttons work, here's how to avoid getting lost:

1. As soon as you get out of your vehicle (or however you arrive at your trailhead), turn on the GPS and mark your location. Use an identifier to ensure you know it is the "home base." Most GPS units have a menu of symbols you can use to identify your marks that are easy to figure out.

2. As you hike, stop periodically and mark your position. These are called "waypoints" and are like dropping crumbs to find your trail back home. Any time I stop to drink, take a picture, or catch my breath, I mark a

waypoint. Most GPS units will have a screen that shows an outline of your route, and this is constructed by your waypoints.

3. If you are hiking into a camp, make sure you mark it as a waypoint when you arrive. Distinguish it as "camp" to avoid confusion.

4. Once you have all these points marked, you can tell the GPS to show you how to get from one selected point to another. The GPS unit will display a directional arrow that will point you exactly where to walk. It's that easy.

More and more people are using GPS units for navigation in the wilderness. That's fine, but I would warn you not to rely on the GPS only. A GPS runs on batteries and utilizes satellite signals. Batteries can run out, and I've been in areas (such as steep, rocky canyons) where the GPS unit can only pick up one satellite, if any at all. This is where your compass and map come in to save the day.

Triangulation

Triangulation involves taking three bearings (azimuths) from your position to distinct land features and charting where they intersect on your map. It can make the difference between being lost and gaining your bearings. It is also invaluable while you are traveling to track your progress and reassure yourself of your position. Having a general idea of your location before you start triangulating is helpful, but that's not absolutely necessary. To ensure the best chance for success, you should start this process from a position that gives you a wide view of the landmarks around you.

STEP 1 – ORIENT YOUR MAP CORRECTLY

Locate a flat, dry surface and spread out your map (use a tarp or poncho on the ground if necessary to protect your map). Find the magnetic declination scale in the bottom margin – TN stands for True North and MN stand for Magnetic North. For this example, it is 9.5 degrees east. A rule to remember is "east is least, west is best." This means that any declination to the east will be subtracted from 360, and any to the west will be added to 360 (remember that the degrees on a compass stop at 360; if you are adding, you would assume 360 as 0). So in this case, a 9.5 degree easterly declination would give us 350.5 (a 9.5 degree westerly deviation would give us 9.5).

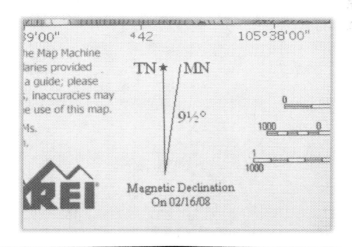

If you are using a base plate compass, rotate the bezel ring until 350.5 lines up with the direction of travel arrow. Now set the straight edge of the compass plate along the edge of the map (or on a line of longitude). Then, with the compass sitting on the map, rotate the map until the north end of the compass needle is "boxed" by the arrow on the bezel ring. The map is now correctly oriented.

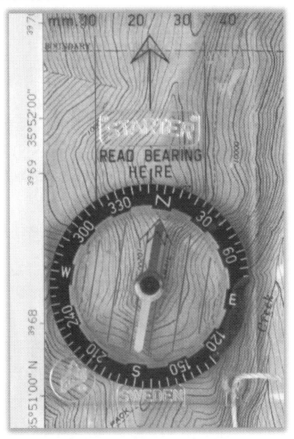

It is wise at this point to weight down the corners of your map so it does not shift.

STEP 2 – IDENTIFY LANDMARKS

Keep the map in front of you. Look into the distance and pick out terrain features that are distinct. Describe them to yourself and imagine what the contour lines would look like as they form the feature on the map. Estimate the distance to the feature.

LARGE, DISTINCT FEATURES ARE BEST TO USE FOR TRIANGULATION

Use a straight stick or a long blade of grass to point at the feature then lower it to the map in front of you, with your "general" location between you and the feature. On the map, look along the line and try to find features that describe what you are looking at.

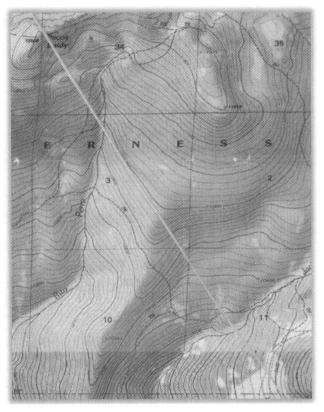

If you see something promising, study it intently and compare all visible aspects of the terrain feature to what you are seeing on the map, *remembering you are only seeing one*

side of it. When you are confident you have identified a landmark, go to the next step.

STEP 3 – SHOOT AZIMUTHS

An azimuth is a bearing (heading) from your location to a distinct land feature, measured in degrees. Some compasses are designed with a sighting lens to shoot very accurate azimuths, but you can still do it with a regular base Keep the compass flat and point it toward the landmark you identified. If it is a base plate compass, rotate the bezel ring until the north arrow lines up with the north end of the needle.

Transfer the compass to your map. Put a forward corner of the base plate on the landmark you identified. Rotate the compass body (not the bezel ring) until the north arrow and the needle line up. Now, draw a line (or use your straight stick/blade of grass) along the straight edge from the landmark toward your position.

Repeat this with two other landmarks, preferably 45 to 60 degrees apart. The three lines will intersect, and you are on to the next step.

STEP 4 – USE TOPOGRAPHY

Examine the area on the map where your three azimuth lines intersect. You are likely in the general area of this intersection, but even a few degrees of error can put you off the mark by several hundred yards or more. Look around you and describe the terrain to yourself. Note the elevation changes, the pitch of the hillsides, any water sources, open areas, or distinct features. Go back to the map and analyze the area around the three intersecting lines. Match up terrain descriptions on the map with what you see around you and pinpoint your location.

Route Selection

The shortest distance between two points is a straight line. It can also be the hardest, most treacherous line you ever walk. Taking a few minutes to study your map and the terrain can get you to your destination faster, with more energy left over, and in one piece.

Using the Terrain to Your Advantage

Once you gain elevation, don't give it up until you are sure of where you are, where you are going, and how you are going to get there. Use the vantage point of a peak or ridge to see the big picture of the terrain you are in. Note the landmarks and look them over closely (they might seem a lot different at another angle, so pick out distinctive features). When it is time to navigate to your next point, visualize a route there that will use natural features to help navigate as well as conserve energy. Examples would be following a ridge instead of bush-whacking through a thick ravine, or following a creek that will lead you right to your destination instead of going straight up and over a steep peak. A direct route might be shorter, but it could be much more taxing. A good rule is, "Work smarter, not harder."

Missing on Purpose

This technique is well-suited for hitting intersections (road, creek, or fence), or finding a vehicle on a road. Example: You are hiking back to your truck, which is parked at a fork in the road about two miles away. You determine a dead-on heading to get there would be 360 degrees (north). The road your truck is parked on is perpendicular to your route. There's a lot of rough terrain between you and your truck, and if you don't hit the intersection exactly, it would be a flip of the coin to know which way to follow the road to find it. Instead, you decide to walk on a 355 heading and hit the road about 100 yards to the west of your truck. You then know to turn right (east) and follow the road to your truck with no guessing.

Negotiating Obstacles

Use this technique when you need to get around a large obstacle, like a swamp, and continue on your heading. Let's start with the assumption that your heading is 270 degrees and the swamp is about 100 yards both long and wide.

1. Add 90 degrees to your heading (360) and follow it far enough to clear the width marsh (keep track of your paces).

2. Turn back onto your original heading (270) and walk far enough to clear the length of the marsh.

3. Subtract 90 degrees from your original course of travel (180) and walk back the same number of paces you counted in step #1. You should be back on your original line of travel, within a few meters or so. Resume your original heading (360) and continue your trek.

A similar technique can be used if you are trying to get around a large obstacle. For instance, you are walking on a heading and find yourself facing a wide valley that is marshy and muddy. Make sure you triangulate your position and know exactly where you are. Draw a line on your current heading, through the marshy valley, and find a definitive terrain feature on the other side. Then, pick a terrain feature that is on heading which completely avoids the valley, but is generally in the same direction you want to go. Walk to that point, and once you get there, shoot a heading to the feature you originally found on the other side of the marshy valley. Sometimes a little extra walking will save you a lot of energy in the long run, not to mention the frustration of difficult obstacles.

Chapter 3 – The Mental Game

Let's fast-forward a bit. You've prepared properly for your trip, and paid attention to what you are doing in the woods. But for whatever reason, you are stuck in the woods and you can't get back to civilization as planned. It could be due to an unexpected storm, a sprained ankle, losing your way in dense timber – you name it. Bottom line: you are stuck.

Fine. Or not? Your mind is going to ask you this question a few times, perhaps yelling it at you. This is the point at which many people turn an unexpected situation into a real emergency in a hurry. How? There are actually a few reasons.

Denial

This is why most people keep walking when they are lost; clinging to the hope that somehow they will stumble into camp or find a familiar landmark. They just can't believe they are lost, and have an "it just doesn't happen to me" sort of mentality. This is dangerous because it never occurs to the person that they are making the situation worse. Additionally, it is harder for searchers to find someone who keeps walking around instead of staying put. Moving around also eats up your energy, can lead to frustration and fear, and generally gets you more stuck. To combat this problem altogether, stop and sit down, take a few deep breaths if you need to, and literally say, "OK, time to switch gears." Then, start dealing with your needs for a night in the woods.

Ego

This is where people know they are lost or stuck, realize they should probably stop for the night, but cannot face the possibility of being the butt of a camp joke or some other kind of teasing. Ego will also cause people to believe they can solve their problem if they just "tough it out" and keep going, instead of stopping to make a shelter for the night. My best advice is: Get over it. So what if you hear a few jokes. You need to act with your brain, not your ego, so you can take care of yourself and get back safely. And trying to be tough can result in your getting hurt, becoming more lost, and finding more trouble. Being tough is a fine trait, but being smart is more advantageous for a survivor.

Panic

Panic can block out all rational thought and flood you with fear of the unknown. It can cause people to run wildly through the woods yelling, or just sit down and cry. Even though it might be the most traumatic mental barrier to deal with, it is also the easiest to defeat. You've already heard me say that preparation leads to confidence. Well, confidence is your weapon for defeating panic. People lose their composure when they feel like they have no control of their destiny, or cannot protect themselves against a threat. You don't fall into that category if you've packed an adequate survival kit, know how to use your survival tools, and have the mindset to take care of yourself.

So let's put you in a scenario: It is a chilly fall afternoon, overcast and breezy, with darkness about 3 hours away. You got turned around on a long hike and estimate you are about 5 miles from your vehicle. You've admitted to yourself you are stuck and stopped to assess your situation. You

have a survival kit and you are not injured. Now
what?

Prioritize

First, ask yourself **WHAT WILL HURT ME
FIRST?** This question will help you set your
priorities. Your needs for survival will be the same
regardless of where or when you get stuck, the
basics being shelter, fire, water, first aid, and
signaling. However, the order in which you
accomplish these is set by your particular
circumstances. First and foremost, you must take
care of any injuries or physical issues that you are
experiencing. Then look at your other needs.
Factors to consider when prioritizing your needs
include:

- Physical condition

- Weather (current and potential)

- Remaining daylight

- How much water and food you have

🌾 How close you are to resources you need, such as dry wood, water, and an area where you can signal rescuers

Once you have an idea of what needs to be done and in what order, take a good look around. See what the environment is giving you to work with. I just spoke about not wandering. But, if you need to move to an area that is protected, or has more abundant resources, don't hesitate. There's a difference. Example: If you are on a hilltop that is exposed, and the wind is starting to howl, drop down into the timber to make your shelter.

In our scenario above, you aren't hurt, so that takes first aid off the table, at least for the short term. What about signaling? If you have a cell phone, a two-way radio, or even a whistle, you might be able to end this situation rather quickly. But, if these are not options (or not effective), then it's on to your physical needs. Based on your circumstances, here's how I would prioritize your actions, and why:

Shelter

The weather is what can hurt you first. Plus, you have darkness approaching. A shelter can take some time to construct depending on what you have with you and the resources available.

Fire

You will need this warmth for the night, and it will act as a signal for any search aircraft. Some might argue a fire is more important than a shelter. A fire won't do you much good if you are sitting in the rain. After you get the shelter constructed, gather enough firewood to last you through the night.

Signal

You can set up some ground-to-air signals first thing in the morning, and they can be working for you while you are meeting other needs.

Water, then food

Hopefully you packed some water and energy food. Regardless, you will need to start looking for a good water source. As time goes on, water will become more important. Don't wait until the need is dire before you start looking for it.

In a very cold environment, you might want to build a fire first so you can warm up periodically as you construct your shelter. In a hot, arid environment, water will work its way higher on your priority list. As I said, different circumstances will have different priorities, but the needs will be the same. So let's start addressing those needs now.

Chapter 4 – Shelter

In my opinion, the key to an effective shelter is simplicity. You need to get protection quickly and with minimal effort. There are exceptions, of course, and sometimes you will have to labor hard to get an adequate shelter constructed. However, it is best to be prepared with materials in your pack that will enable to get you out of the elements and comfortable for the night without worry.
Regardless of what materials you use or how long it will take you to build, the effort is futile if you don't first pick a safe, adequate site for your shelter.

Site Selection

Consider the general topography of where you are. Valleys and drainages will be where cold air collects, but the tops of hills will be more exposed to the wind. Avoid the bottoms of ravines or dry creek beds, especially in arid country, due to the possibility of flash floods. Make sure you have the necessary resources close at hand to build what you need (framework, bough bed, etc). If you have the time to deliberate on a location, remember that south facing slopes (in North America) will get more sunlight and generally have more sparse trees. North-facing slopes will get more shade and generally have dense tree cover. Once you have selected the general area where you will build a shelter, narrow your focus.

Look for an area that is flat, level and large enough for you to build your shelter. This means, at a minimum, a place that is big enough for you to lie down comfortably. Avoid soft, damp, or muddy ground if possible. Be wary of anthills, bee hives, and game trails, as they will all be a problem if you build a shelter on or near them. Clear the area of snow, rocks, and debris, and beware of overhead hazards (such as large, dead branches and dead or leaning trees that can crash down in wind or snow). Once you've found a good site, you're ready to construct a shelter.

Simple Knots

Before you start constructing a shelter, it will help to know a few common knots, lashes and hitches.

Clove Hitch

This hitch utilizes friction to hold tension. It is excellent for tying to stakes or ending a lash.

1

2

3

4

Timber Hitch

This hitch utilizes friction to hold tension. It is a good "anchor" lash for attaching line to a pole when starting a lash.

1

2

3

Cow Hitch

This hitch is most effective for attaching line to the grommets of a tarp without having to tie a knot. It is especially useful in cold or snowy environments where untying a knot would be difficult.

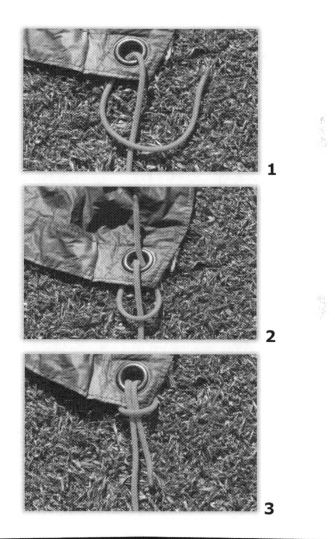

Square Knot

This knot is used for connecting two pieces of rope that are approximately the same diameter or thickness.

1

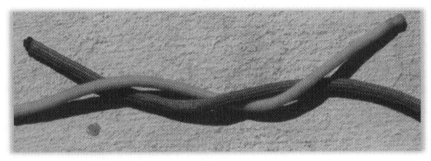

2

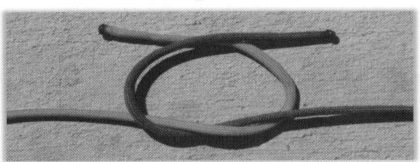

3

4

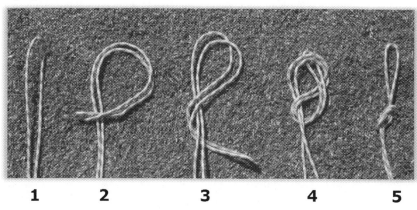

5

Figure Eight

This is a fast, simple way to put a fixed loop in a rope, either at the end or in the middle.

1 **2** **3** **4** **5**

Common Shelter Designs

Lean-to

Utilizing a Tarp

A lean-to is quick and easy, and I often carry an Army-style poncho in my hunting pack for just such an occasion (they are waterproof and the corners have reinforced grommets for securing rope or stakes). You can also use nylon tarps, which are available in most sporting goods stores, as well as heavyweight "sportsman's blankets" that are silver on one side and colored on the other. The sportsman's blankets reflect heat well if you put a fire in front of your shelter, and they usually weigh a little less than an Army poncho. Regardless of the material, the steps to build it are the same:

1. Select a site between two trees (or other structures) 6-8 feet apart.

2. Secure two corners of one side of the tarp to the trees/structures about 3-4 feet off the ground.

3. Pull the remaining two corners out at a 45-60 degree angle and tie them off to stakes, rocks, etc. It's better to pull the material tight and eliminate as many wrinkles as possible – this will help shed precipitation. If you plan to use a fire, orient your shelter so the wind does not blow directly in, but rather at 90 degrees to the opening.

4. If you anticipate heavy precipitation (and time permitting), reinforce the shelter by using a ridge pole lashed 3-4 feet off the ground between the trees and lean a few support poles against it at a 45 degree angle, then stretch your tarp over the frame.

5. An easy way to anchor a tarp that does not have grommets in the corners is to make a "button." Create a slip knot in the end of a piece of rope. Gather a small pinch (no bigger than a golf ball) of dirt or duff in your fingers and fold the corner of the material over it. Now pinch the wad from the outside of the

material and pass the slip knot over it, tightening at the bottom (the wad of dirt or duff will now look like a small balloon in the material).

ILLUSTRATION OF A "BUTTON" – A WAY TO ATTACH A ROPE TO A SHELTER PIECE IF THERE IS NO GROMMET

Utilizing Natural Material

It will be necessary to construct a framework for this shelter. Select a site as described above. Then locate a sturdy, straight ridgepole a little longer than the space between your trees. Tie the ends of the ridgepole to each tree – the height is a personal preference, but I try not to get it higher than 4 feet. You need to test the ridgepole for strength – it should support your weight. This is necessary to ensure the structure will withstand not only the weather but also the weight of the materials you will be adding soon.

Next, find sturdy poles and lean them against the ridgepole at a 45 degree angle. An easy way to figure this out accurately is to measure the distance between the ridgepole and the ground directly beneath. Then measure the same distance from beneath the ridgepole and scribe a line in the dirt parallel to the ridgepole. As you lay the support poles across the ridgepole and onto the ground, put the butt ends on the line you scribed in the dirt. The more poles you lay on the better. At this point, if you have thin, flexible branches, you can weave them between the support poles (perpendicular to them) and create a lattice-work of sorts.

Now add thatching, whatever it may be. Pine boughs work very well and you place them butt-end first (jam the butt between the poles) and overlap them like shingles, meaning you start placing the boughs at the bottom of the shelter and work toward the ridgepole. You can also use slabs of bark, bundles of cattail stalks, broad leafy branches, you name it. The idea is to add enough thatching to the framework that you cannot see light through it when sitting inside the shelter. As you might imagine, this can take a lot of material. Once the protection is adequate, you can enclose the sides if you want (use more poles and thatching in the same way as described above).

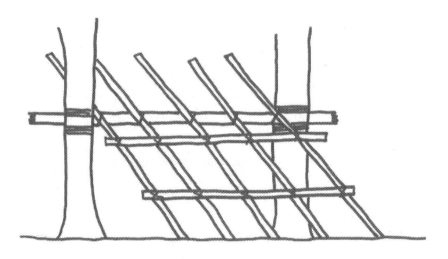

A STURDY LEAN-TO FRAME – YOU COULD PUT A TARP ON IT NOW, OR ADD MORE CROSS POLES TO PREPARE FOR NATURAL MATERIALS

You can expand on a lean-to be creating two lean-tos sharing the same ridge pole (facing each other). It gives you more room and more protection from overhead weather, plus it cuts the wind well. Figure on twice the time, resources, and effort to get this built. I tried to construct one during my instructor training graduation exercise. I was alone and started building at about 10:00 AM. At dark, I was still working. I was running short on pine boughs and basically had a good lean-to with a semi-thatched front covering. It was comfortable and I improved on it each day. By the end of the exercise it was pretty solid and it kept me completely dry in the rain.

A-frame

Utilizing a Tarp

Plastic paint drop cloths make great emergency shelters. They are lighter and cheaper than tarps or ponchos, and you might even have on in the garage already. Otherwise, you can find them in a hardware store for a couple dollars. They come in various sizes and weights – you want at least 2-mil thickness and preferably 8′ X 10′ in size. Here's how to use it:

1. In a hurry, you can tie a rope to the trunk of a tree 3-4 feet off the ground. Pull it very tight and stake out the other end (or tie it to a stump, rock etc) 8-9 feet away.

2. Stretch your tarp over the line with even lengths on either side. At the "opening" (the highest point, closest to the anchor tree). Using a grommet or a button to attach a line to the middle of the tarp above the "door" of the shelter, then tie it to the tree (give yourself 1-2 feet of room between the opening of the shelter and the tree).

3. At the bottom end of the shelter, pull of the middle of the tarp (over your ridgeline) and stake it, making sure the material is tight.

4. Now, starting at the "opening" of the shelter, pull out each corner at 45 degrees to the ridgeline and stake. Work your way to the back of the shelter, alternating sides as you stake out the material and eliminating as many wrinkles as possible.

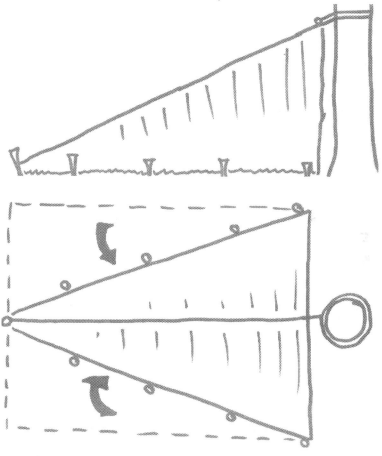

5. You can also construct a framework by lashing a ridgepole to the anchor tree instead of using rope.

6. If you are not using an anchor tree, you can create a tripod, with one leg being long, and stretch the tarp over the frame.

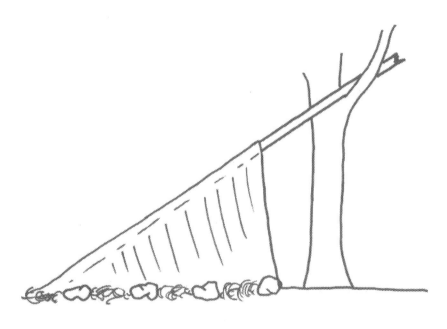

A-FRAME SHELTER USING A TARP AND UTILIZING SOLID RIDGEPOLE AND ROCKS TO STAKE OUT THE EDGES

Utilizing Natural Material

It is time-consuming to construct and requires adequate material, but I've slept through a snowstorm in my t-shirt using this shelter because of its excellent ability to trap body heat.

The shelter you build will be small in order to utilize your body heat. I like to find a good site in thick stands of pine trees so I can utilize the windbreak and available building resources. Clear the ground to bare earth.

You will need a sturdy ridgepole, 8 to 10 feet long, to start construction. Next, look for a strong branch or crook that's three to four feet off the ground. If this isn't available, sometimes you can find two trees close together where you can wedge the ridgepole up at the same height. Even better still, you might find a fallen tree that is set up in a similar way. No matter what, make sure the ridge pole is anchored securely and test its strength; it should support your weight. Clear the branches and stobs off the underside of the ridgepole. Imagine the ridgepole as a spine. Now line both sides with as many "ribs" as possible, keeping them tightly spaced and angled at about 45 degrees from ridge to ground.

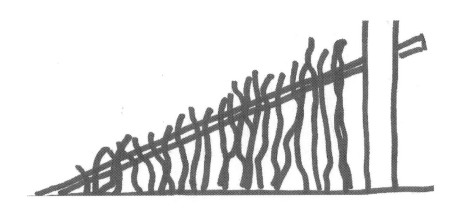

Cover this framework with whatever you have available: pine boughs (shingle them), dead leaves and pine needles (heap it on), snow, or even dirt and sod.

Make your covering thick enough that you can't see any gaps of light when you crawl in.

Find as much insulating material as possible (make sure it is dry): pine needle duff, dead leaves, pine boughs, grass, etc. Line the floor of the shelter with a THICK layer and pack it into the foot area. Pile up as much as possible right at the entrance to your shelter, and find a few more "ribs." Crawl in feet first and start packing the insulating material in around your body. Cover yourself up, too. Leave a comfortable (physically and mentally) space around your head for access to the outside and breathing. Reach out and prop up the remaining "ribs" to enclose the entrance and hold in your insulation. Rearrange and find a comfortable position. The insulation around you will form a cocoon of dead air space to keep you warm. The roof above you will block the elements and hold in your body heat.

Wiki-up

Perhaps you are in an area where trees sturdy enough to use for any of the shelters above are not common, or ridgepoles and boughs are not available. This is a situation I often encounter on hikes throughout New

Mexico. An efficient and easy shelter design commonly used is called a Wiki-up. Picture a tripod with each leg approximately 8 feet long. These legs can be made from any type of wood you find, even if it isn't straight. The stronger the better, but sometimes you have to make do with what you've got. Pick a side of the tripod that will be your "door" and start laying any branches or woods you can find into the tripod on the other two sides, maintaining a circular pattern with the butt ends on the ground. Feel free to set in as many branches as you want – the denser the better. Now add thatching, using the technique and materials described in shelters above. In the end, you will have something that looks like a squat tipi with an open doorway.

Caves

Caves are perhaps the simplest shelter because they don't require construction. They are, in my opinion, the least consistent because finding them is often by chance. There are places in the southwest where you can crawl around canyons and rimrock with a fairly good chance of finding a decent cave. But if you are in survival mode and needing to worry about other needs at the same time, banking your money on finding a cave is probably not a safe bet. In terrain such as I described, you will almost always find some sort of overhang or protected area that will suffice.

If you do find a cave, make sure it is not being inhabited by another life form. Avoid the temptation to go exploring if the cave is deep – geologic formations can be unstable and you don't need to go getting yourself in more a predicament than you are already in.

AN EXCELLENT EXAMPLE OF A SHALLOW CAVE SHELTER

If you are using a fire, keep it as near the opening as possible to allow for proper venting. In some cases, the fire might need to be moved directly outside the opening to keep the cave from filling with smoke. If the rock is wet or frozen a fire will likely cause it to crack, pop, or explode (the moisture in the rock is super-heated and the expanding water vapor generates a lot of pressure – take precautions).

Remember also that rock will conduct heat away from your body, so it is important to use an insulation bed (see "Insulation Bed" below).

Tree Well

Very fast and very effective, a tree well is nothing more than the area around the trunk of a tree (preferably a pine tree) where the ground is most protected by the overhead branches. The branches on coniferous (needle-bearing) trees will act as an umbrella of sorts. I've ducked under the lower boughs of pine trees many times on rainy hikes. Not only are you protected, but so are the dry, dead branches that tend to clump around the lower trunk of pine trees. In this way, you are meeting two needs at once (A few words of caution: don't build your fire under the branches of the tree, and be wary of using a tree well if you are on a high ridge or other elevated position due to lightening concerns). If the environment is snowy, a tree well is even more pronounced and will sometimes feel like a cove or bathtub because the snow slides off the branches above and builds up like walls around the base. This adds an insulator to your quick shelter, but body heat can start to melt and weaken the snow above. This can lead to an unexpected dollop of icy slush hitting you when you least expect, or worse, a big chunk of snow breaking loose and showering down on you. You can improve on a tree well at any time of year because it has so much natural protection already present, but remember the safety issues described above.

Creativity

These examples aren't meant to say that you can only use one kind of material or another. Creativity and improvising are the hallmarks of effective survival. You can build a lean-to framework from sturdy poles and cover it with a plastic sheet or poncho plus boughs, or stuff dry leaves into a garbage bag to make a loftier insulation bed. Use what you have and make your shelter as strong and efficient as possible. Add to it each chance you get. You sometimes trade off strength for speed when dealing with immediate action shelters. If the storm passes and you are going to spend more time in the shelter, add strength and reinforcement to it so the protection and durability will be extended. The possibilities are limited only by your imagination. It is, as the saying goes, just common sense.

Insulation Bed

Sleeping directly on the ground can be cold and uncomfortable. To better your rest, try the following:

1. Spread a layer of pine boughs inside your shelter. Push the stob-ends into the ground at an angle, so the boughs hump slightly. Work from one end of your mattress to the other, using a shingle effect and ensuring all boughs are pointing in the same direction.

2. Cover the first layer with a second layer of boughs, this time laying them in the opposite direction, and interlace the layers as you go. Fill-in gaps with smaller pieces to maximize comfort.

3. Your mattress will create a barrier of dead air space between your body and the ground (just like an inflatable sleeping pad), and dead air space equals warmth. You can also use other available material, such as leaves or brush, as long as it accomplishes the same objective.

Chapter 5 - Fire

One of the most critical survival skills to know when venturing into the wilderness is fire-building. Fire itself is useful for warmth, cooking, purifying water, signaling, drying wet clothes, and mental comfort, to name a few. There are many, many ways to get a fire going and keep it going, but for our purposes, we want to build a fire as fast and easy as possible. That means some techniques, such as using friction with a bow and drill, are not the best choice. I know a few people who can get a fire going with a bow and drill as fast as you can read this, but they learned how over years of practice and guidance from experienced instructors. I want you to be able to start a fire right away, as soon as you put this book down. Therefore, I've narrowed the techniques to fast and simple rules that are easy to learn.

As with any skill, it is best to start by learning the basics – how a fire "works." The easiest way to illustrate this principle is the fire triangle: Heat, Oxygen, and Fuel. The ratio between these three sides of the triangle causes the chemical reaction needed to create flames and keep them going. You must maintain a careful balance between these three factors. Too much of one, or not enough of the other, and you will not get your fire built.

Heat

This is what gets the fire going and keeps it going. It can start as a match, a spark, a cigarette lighter, an ember from a bow and drill – you name it. As a responsible outdoor enthusiast, you will carry at least two, preferably three ways to create this heat. Once this heat takes root in tinder (explained below), you will have flames ready to burn fuel.

Oxygen

For flames to grow, they need a healthy supply of oxygen. This is why we incorporate a brace in the fire building process, and I'll explain more about it as we go along. If we piled fuel on a small flame, we could snuff it out. A brace allows us to prop the fuel up over the flame, giving it room to eat and grow.

Fuel

What you build your fire with will have a direct bearing on how successful you are. The key words to remember are: *long, lean,* and *dry,* meaning that you want a heap of long, slender pieces of bone-dry wood for the flames to eat up. A few minutes of searching for good fuel can save a lot of time when it comes to actually building a fire.

This reminds me of my first fire building test when I was an instructor trainee. There was about 2 feet of snow on the ground and it was cold in northeastern Washington. We had the task of building a split wood fire, which meant we had to take down a tree with our axe and render it into small pieces for fuel. I ran into the forest and took a tree apart fast, breaking it into beautiful stages of kindling. Then, I spent the next hour trying to get the wood to burn. It got dark and the snow started to fall. Everyone else was done except me. Then, in a moment of clarity, one of our instructors looked closely at my fuel. It was green wood from a live tree. The cold made the wood brittle, so it acted like it was dead and dry. But I hadn't looked carefully enough. I spent the next hour rebuilding a fire in the dark, and in the end I was absolutely exhausted. I got a fire going, but I failed the test. I was devastated, but I learned (the hard way) to always double check the fuel source to make sure it is adequate.

FIRE BUILDING IN 6 STEPS

STEP 1 – FUEL SELECTION

An obvious place to start is finding the wood you will burn...your fuel. There are many sources, but three which are generally found everywhere in forested areas, easy to access, and easy to convert to fire: dead branches, a dead tree that is still standing, and stumps. Each has an advantage and a disadvantage. Let's look at them in order:

Dead Branches

This is perhaps the easiest source of fuel for you to get at. You are looking for branches that:

🌿 Don't have any green vegetation on them

❧ Bark is missing or slipping off in places

❧ Gray, brittle, and dry

An excellent place to search is under the thick boughs of fir and spruce trees. The upper branches act as umbrellas and keep the branches clustered at the base of the trunk dry. Branches found there tend to be smaller and look like big spider webs. This is perfect, because a fire needs small, combustible fuel first and usually in greater quantities. If you find the right tree, you can load up with plenty left to come back for.

Some trees, like Ponderosa pines, tend to have less dense branches that are thicker in diameter, which makes them more exposed to precipitation. Generally speaking, these branches need to be broken down into smaller pieces before they will help you get a fire going (see the discussion of splitting wood with a knife in "Breaking Fuel into Stages" below – it works the same way for big branches).

Deciduous (leaf-bearing) trees can be tricky since they lose their green leaves in the fall and winter and can seem brittle in very cold weather. However, green trees will have limbs that are slightly springy if you bend them, and scraping the outer bark will show a green or yellow layer underneath. Avoid this and seek branches that have no bark or buds and snap crisply when bent.

A note on dead branches – some will have sloughing bark that is damp or wet. Strip this off as you prepare it and it will save you from a smoking, smoldering pile of branches. The bark is only good as a sponge at this point, and that will not help our fire. If the wood is damp, it will dry quickly after added to an established fire.

GATHER ENOUGH FUEL TO EASILY START YOUR FIRE AND KEEP IT GOING

Dead Standing Trees

Dead standing trees are a good source for dry wood, even in wet weather, because they have less surface area to catch precipitation. Even if the outer side is wet, the inner heart wood will be dry. But a critical step is to select the right tree, as my story earlier in the chapter pointed out. Keys to look for are:

🌿 No signs of green vegetation

🌿 Peeling or sloughing bark on the trunk

🌿 A hollow sound when thumped

Often, the tree will have weak roots and can be pushed over. Obviously, a hatchet or small axe is very handy for breaking up this fuel source. If you have an axe, I would limit the search to a trunk diameter similar to a softball, or smaller. But if you have only a knife or compact saw, look for trees that are no larger than a soda can in diameter. By using leverage, rocks, and whatever else is available, you can break up a tree this size into manageable size pieces, ideally about two feet in length.

Stumps

It's not uncommon to see rotting stumps and root spikes poking up around the forest from dead coniferous (pine) trees. If it is a flat-topped stump cut by a chainsaw, it probably won't help you much. They catch a lot of water and are generally tough to cut into. However, if the tree deteriorated naturally, there is probably a solid stump left that you can pull pieces off of and split up. If you find one that looks promising, give it a kick. If it is solid, split off a piece and cut into it. You want to avoid anything that looks crumby, rotten, or punky. You can break it up by hand and with a knife by the method described below. If the wood has a streaky, translucent discoloration between the grains ranging from yellow to purple and smells strongly of pine, you've likely found pitch wood. This is better still, as pitch wood is highly combustible and will burn in the toughest conditions.

Other Sources

Dead wood that is lying on the ground is an option, but only if the environment is dry. Otherwise, the wood acts as a sponge to any moisture on the ground or in the air. Dead logs are often punky and rotten inside, and using this kind of wood is a waste of time. There are also trees that have fallen over from wind, struck by lightning, or otherwise shattered. This is a great chance to pull apart long pieces of wood which will split up nicely and save a lot of work.

STEP 2 – SITE SELECTION

Once you've found an adequate supply of fuel, look for a good site to build your fire. If you are constructing a camp, you will have some time to plan the layout. If you are trying to get flames for a dire reason, you won't have time as a luxury.

In bad weather, look for a spot that is sheltered from wind and precipitation. This can be under a rock ledge, in a thicket of pine saplings, or under the high branches of a big tree. However, in a snowy environment, avoid building you fire under the branches of a tree. Few examples illustrate the importance of this rule better than what takes place in the short story, "*To Build a Fire*" by Jack London. In this story, a man in the wilds of Alaska during winter finds himself in a precarious situation and has to build a fire to save his life. He builds the fire under a spruce tree that was covered in snow. As he warms up and congratulates himself for being a great woodsman, the snow in the boughs above him melts enough to come showering down on him and his fire. I don't want to ruin the story, but let's say this is a turning point in the man's adventure. Once you find the right site, clear the area down to bare soil, at least 3 feet in diameter. This will prevent the fire from spreading.

STEP 3 – PLATFORM AND BRACE

A platform will serve as a barrier against damp or wet earth and it is especially necessary when the soil is frozen or covered with ice. One effective way to get material for a platform is to pull a thick sheet of bark off a dead tree or stump (twelve inches square is a good size). Lay the outer surface of the bark on the ground and use the dry inner surface to build your fire on. You can also build a platform from dry branches or pieces of dry split wood. Again, make sure the platform is big enough to work on (12" square being the minimum). A note – depending on the tinder you are using, a platform built from branches or split might let it fall through the cracks.

A SHEET OF THICK BARK PULLED OFF A STUMP MAKES A GREAT PLATFORM, AND THE INNER SURFACE WILL USUALLY BE DRY

A brace is something that you will lean your fuel against, rather than building a teepee of sticks. Believe me, it saves time and is more efficient once the flame is lit. Look for a larger stick or piece of wood that is 3"or so in diameter – about the feel of a pop can in your hand. Then lay the brace across your platform.

STEP 4 - BREAKING FUEL INTO STAGES

Take the fuel you've collected and break it into three groups, or stages. The first should be pieces that are about the size of chopsticks to the size of a pencil – very thin. You want to have at least three big handfuls of this size. The second stage should be between the size of your pinky finger and your thumb. The last stage is anything larger than your thumb. The really big chunky pieces should be set aside for later, when the fire is roaring along. They won't help it get built right now.

Breaking fuel into stages could be as simple as snapping branches. But for split wood or wood from stumps, there are other options.

If your knife is a stout fixed blade model, you can use it as a splitting wedge of sorts.

1. Place one end of the piece of wood on the ground or platform and stand it upright with one hand

2. Place the blade, sharp side down, on the top of the piece - if the piece has a natural crack or split in the grain, line up the blade with it

3. Using a heavy stick, tap the back (blunt) edge of your knife blade and drive it down into the wood. As the blade buries in the wood, tap on the front end of the blade that is exposed as you push downward on the handle, and work the knife down through the wood. The pieces will pop apart as you get closer to the bottom. Repeat the process with the halves, quarters, and so on.

As the pieces split off, don't let them lay on the ground – this will expose the heart wood to moisture, which it will suck up quickly. Find a platform of some sort to put them on, or prop them against a log or tree. If you don't have a fixed blade knife, you can use flat rocks as wedges and pound them into the cracks of a piece of wood to get a rough split.

As the pieces get smaller, you can use the tip of a knife blade as a splitting tool, as well. Find a solid base to work on and lay down a long, lean piece of split wood, grasping the end closest to you. Then, with the sharp edge facing away from your hand, press the tip of the knife blade into the wood between the grains and twist it back and forth gently. I don't advise using a folding knife to do this unless it has a locking blade. Even then, be sure to avoid accidently having the blade close on your fingers. The wood will pop apart, and you can repeat this process until the pieces are toothpick size in diameter if need be. If you don't have a knife, you can pound the length of a thin piece of split wood with a rock and fracture into many smaller pieces.

BREAKING FUEL INTO THREE STAGES AND PROTECTING IT FROM GROUND MOISTURE BY USING A PLATFORM

As you are breaking your fuel down into smaller and smaller stages, I would recommend you make a few handfuls of shavings. They are highly combustible and will help the flame from your tinder get bigger and hotter FAST so your fire will take off. Here's how to do it:

1. Find a dry, straight piece of wood that's about 12" long and 1" in diameter

2. Place one end on a solid base and hold the other end firmly. Using a sharp knife and cutting away from your body, slice the blade into the wood at a very shallow angle and cut down the length of the stick. You should see a thin feather of wood begin to peel off and curl

3. Cut all the way to the base of the stick and let the wood shaving fall off. It is wise to have something to catch the shavings in, such as your hat or a ground cloth to protect them from moisture

4. Repeat until you have two or three handfuls of shavings. You can also leave the shavings attached to the stick, whichever you prefer.

STEP 5 – PREPARE TINDER

After you get your fuel broken into stages, you need to prepare tinder. Good tinder will light with a spark and it will burn strong. It has to hold a flame long enough for your smallest stages of kindling to ignite. Tinder can be sensitive to moisture and shouldn't come out until the last minute.

Man-Made Tinder

As a prepared outdoor enthusiast, you should carry enough tinder in your survival kit to easily start three fires. There are many types available commercially. If you buy a firestarter, experiment with it, be sure you can get it lit, and make sure it lives up to expectations. If it does not, find something that will. Through years of trial and error, I have come up with the good, the not-so-good, the ugly, and the "ultimate." You might come up with your own, but this can be a place to start.

The Good

Ultimate Survival Technologies makes a product called WetFire tinder, and it is the best I've found on the market. It takes a spark quickly (crush it first by pinching it with your fingers), it burns in any condition, and it has a long, hot flame. They are also small and lightweight.

The Not-So-Good

Magnesium bars seem to be a prevalent item marketed as a firestarter. Most are small, keychain-size affairs with a flint striker on one side. The idea is to shave a pile of magnesium scrapings off one side, then light them with a spark from the flint. Shaving enough magnesium for tinder can take a while. Plus, gathering the magnesium shavings into a neat little pile in field conditions can be challenging at best. However, magnesium does take a spark and burns hot. But this is what I would call "flash tinder" because it does not last more than a few seconds.

The Ugly

There are a few pastes and liquids on the market, and I advise avoiding them for your survival kit. They can be messy, and if a container or tube breaks, they will wreak havoc on your pack and other survival kit items. Most are made with a petroleum product and a stabilizer, both of which will ruin nylon and plastic. They are great for starting the BBQ grill, but not for packing in the woods.

The "Ultimate"

Take about two dozen cotton balls, saturate them with petroleum jelly, and store them in a plastic baggie or 35mm film canister. When it's time to light a fire, take out two or three saturated cotton balls and pull them apart at the edges until there are greasy fibers sticking out in all directions. This tinder will light readily with a spark, and one cotton ball will burn between four and five minutes. It's the best tinder I've used...period. It has performed in all weather conditions, in all situations, flawlessly. Plus, it is inexpensive and simple to make.

COTTONBALLS SATURATED WITH PETROLEUM JELLY (LEFT); ULTIMATE SURVIVAL'S WETFIRE TINDER (RIGHT)

Others

Most grocery stores have an isle where you can find picnic supplies. Somewhere in there I usually see the "fake logs" used to burn in fireplaces or smaller such items to start BBQ briquettes. They are normally inexpensive, and if you cut them into pieces about 1" square, you will have a tinder source for many fires. These burn best if lit with a flame (match or lighter). If you are going to use a spark, chop or shave the tinder piece into flaky bits before you try to light it.

A PLATFORM AND BRACE WITH TINDER READY TO IGNITE (COTTONBALL SATURATED WITH PETROLEUM JELLY)

Natural Tinder

It is good to know natural sources of tinder, but don't rely totally on them – take something with you in your kit. However, if you come across one of the items described below, take advantage of it.

Pine Pitch

Dead pine trees often have pitch-impregnated wood in the stumps. It is highly flammable and will light even if it's been submerged in water. On one of my training trips to the coast of Oregon, I found a piece of driftwood that was loaded with pitch – who knows how long it had been floating in the bay. I made a pile of shavings and it lit on the first try. If you find pitch wood, try this technique for preparing it as tinder:

1. Get a long, straight piece that is that is about 1" in diameter and clean it up so you have a flat surface to work with. Place one end of the pitch stick on a solid base and hold the other end firmly

2. Set the sharp edge of your knife blade on the flat surface at 90 degrees and press into the stick. Scrape the blade away from you, using your thumb on the blade for leverage, and stroke the length of the stick. You should see small, fluffy shavings peel off the wood

3. Repeat until you have a big handful

NOTE: It is common to see gobs of dried sap on the outer bark of pine trees. It will burn in this form, but it does not take a spark well. Exposure to a flame for several seconds will usually get it lit.

PREPARING PITCH WOOD FOR TINDER

Birch Bark

Birch trees often have shreds of bark peeling off them, and they make great tinder. They take a flame readily, but getting them to take a spark means preparing the bark further. Wad several strips into a ball and rub vigorously between your hands. Break the bark down into fibers and make a nest for the spark.

BIRCH BARK

Goat's Beard

This lichen (sometimes referred to as Old Man's Beard or Witch's Hair) can be found hanging in large skeins from coniferous trees in many western forests. The lichen is very fibrous and has the consistency and feel of a kitchen scrub pad: somewhat bristly and firm, but easily wadded into a large ball. Since it hangs freely from branches, it catches any breeze and available sunlight which means it is often dry. However, if there is any moisture in the air, it will soak it up like a sponge. When dry, it will take a spark easily and burn well – use a softball sized wad at a minimum for starting your kindling.

GOAT'S BEARD

Inner Bark of Deciduous Trees

The layer of bark between the heart wood and the rough outer bark, called the cambium layer, is where a deciduous tree holds a lot of water and nutrients. When a tree dies, the cambium layer will dry out. As the outer layer of bark begins to slough, you can peel away slabs and expose the dry inner bark. It pulls away from the inside of the rough outer bark in paper-thin strips. Wad up a handful of these, rub them vigorously between the palms of your hands, and make a nest. It will take a spark well – my personal favorite is the inner bark from a cottonwood tree.

STRIPS OF INNER BARK FROM A DEAD COTTONWOOD TREE

Others

Dead grass, leaves, and pine needles are often referred to as being good tinder. They are better lit with a flame than with a spark, and they will burn well. Grasses and leaves are sensitive to moisture, and are often found on the ground, so conditions need to be ideal for you to use them. Lighting pine needles themselves (such as a large handful of needles found at the base of a tree) can be difficult, even with a sustained flame, as they tend to clump and eliminate the oxygen needed to burn well. When still attached to a branch, dead pine needles will take a flame and build it up well with a rush of crackling and snapping. I prefer to add these to tinder after it is burning as a way to get the flames going fast.

IGNITION SOURCES

Wooden Matches

There are many "waterproof" wooden matches on the market, but I've found none that live up to expectations. "Strike on the box" wooden matches require the specific striker found on the box to get them lit. If the striker is wet or gets mangled, you are out of luck. The "strike anywhere" matches that have a white sulfur tip are very reliable and you can scratch them on almost anything to get them lit. Whatever you chose, keep them in a watertight container. You can get an inexpensive screw-top model at the local military surplus store (just make sure it has a rubber gasket on the cap). You can also wrap them in a plastic baggie and rubber band, or dip them completely in paraffin. Carry at least a dozen, preferably more.

Lighters

Regular cigarette lighters are fine, and they even come in mini sizes for small kits. My favorite lighter is a weatherproof model made by Brunton called the Helios. It looks like a tank and is larger than a standard lighter. However, it has rubber gaskets, a locking lid, and it lights like a small torch. You can refill the Helios with fuel (butane) and adjust the size of the flame. It lights in any weather and wind does not affect the flame – something a normal lighter cannot compare to.

Metal Match

A metal match can also be referred to as "fire steel," but it is basically the same sort of sparking product found in most cigarette lighters – just larger. A metal match is impervious to water and wind and it will last for literally thousands of strikes (depending on the size, of course). You can use any sharp-edged striker, but knife blades or metal shanks similar to a section of hacksaw blade seem to work best.

Set the tip of the metal match (end away from your grip hand) onto a firm surface (the platform, in this case). Put the edge of your striker at 90 degrees to the surface of the metal match, push into the metal match slightly, and stroke the striker down the length of the metal match. Hot sparks will flare off the metal match and generally fall in the area at the base (near the tip) of the metal match. This is where your tinder should be. It takes a little practice, but I've seen people master this tool in a matter of minutes.

METAL MATCH WITH STRIKER (LEFT), STRIKE-ANYWHERE MATCHES IN WATERPROOF CONTAINER (RIGHT), STORM-PROOF LIGHTER (BOTTOM; BRUNTON HELIOS)

STEP 6 – PUTTING IT ALL TOGETHER

Once you've lit your tinder, the next step is to give the flame something to eat. If you've made shavings, gently add a handful to the flame now. If not, or after the flame has caught them, take a good handful of the smallest (thinnest) fuel pieces you have and lay them across the brace and over the flame, so they sit at a 45 degree angle.

PHOTO BY HEATHER SOLOMON

When you lay these pieces down, fan them out like a deck of cards before you set them across the flame so there is plenty of room for the flame to work up through the wood. The brace and the spaces between the fuel pieces ensure there is plenty of oxygen present for the flame. As the flame grows stronger, move up in size through your fuel stages, fanning out the pieces as you lay them across the brace. If the flame has a hard time growing, stay at the smaller stages until it is strong enough.

PHOTO BY HEATHER SOLOMON

Building a Solid Foundation

All of this work pays off rather quickly and, if done correctly, you will have a tall, crackling blaze in a minute or two. They key now is to keep the fire going and build it to suit your needs. Remember, the larger the piece of wood, the slower it will burn. So if you drag big logs onto the fire, the flame size will probably decrease and the noticeable light and heat will decrease as well. The flip side to this is smaller limbs and fuel pieces require you to be monitoring the fire closely and staying on top of things. This is one key reason why it is important to have more than enough fuel gathered before you try to start your fire – you don't want to be scrambling around trying to find more dry wood to feed a flame that isn't established yet. Once you get a solid base of red-hot glowing coals, you can breathe a little easier.

Reflectors

Using a fire to stay warm for the night is a primary purpose, and there are ways to make it more effective. We will discuss reflectors below, but the size of the fire is also important. The size and layout of your shelter are key considerations (as well as what it's made of). A long, open shelter like a lean-to would benefit from a longer fire and reflector in front. If you are in a cave, a smaller fire with a focused reflector should do the trick well. Most people build their fires much larger than are necessary. It might feel empowering, but it is mostly just a waste of fuel. Keep it small and efficient.

You need to utilize as much of the fire's heat as possible. A fire is putting off heat and light in all directions – you are only exposed to a small portion of it. A reflector will redirect some of that escaping heat and light back at you. Your shelter is also a reflector of sorts and will help contain and concentrate heat as well.

A simple reflector that most people see in books and magazines is a long wall of stacked poles. This works well, but it does require some effort. Building it with green wood is recommended, but anything will do in a pinch. Build the reflector on the opposite side of your fire from your shelter, parallel to the opening of your shelter. Place it about 2 feet from the fire itself. Start by sinking long stakes into the ground and angle them back away from the fire slightly. Next, stack the reflector poles against the supports, biggest poles on the bottom, and go at least 3 feet high. If necessary, you can lash them to the supports.

Another type of reflector is made from rocks. The most important thing to remember is not to use wet or frozen rocks – they can and will explode if heated. Some places have great slabs of flat rock that can be set on their sides. My favorite way to construct one is to make it horseshoe shaped for maximum efficiency. A downside is you usually can't stack the rocks very high, but it is quick to build.

A QUICK PONCHO LEAN-TO WITH A FIRE REFLECTOR CONSTRUCTED OF ROCKS. TOTAL TIME TO BUILD: 20 MINUTES.

Chapter 6 – Water

Our bodies are composed largely of water, and we can lose a lot of it during a day in the woods. Sweating, urinating, and just breathing all eliminate moisture from our bodies, and it is essential to replenish it at a regular pace. The goal is to avoid dehydration, which can happen even in mild weather but alarmingly fast in hot or strenuous conditions. Dehydration can cause (among other symptoms) fatigue, nausea, and poor judgment.

To prevent this, carry a supply of water with you (some might call it burdensome, but I consider two quarts a minimum) and drink it throughout the day. Unfortunately, water can be a heavy, awkward commodity, especially for people who are hiking into the backcountry. Take a look in any sporting goods catalog and you will see many creative ways to carry a day's supply of water, and the choice is largely personal preference. But more importantly, have the means to collect water in the field and make it safe to drink.

Open Sources

A basic rule of survival is to stay put if you get lost, but you may need to relocate if you don't have a water source available. Two things to look for when trying to find water are: low-lying areas (like the bottom of a ravine) and lush, green vegetation. Cattails and waterfowl are also a good indicator that water is nearby. These indicators can lead you to "traditional" open sources of water, such as ponds and creeks. But there are many other open sources, some of which you might walk pass or dismiss initially.

If you locate standing water, such as a swamp or backwater, it may look and smell unpleasant, but it's still water. If it's all you have, you need to make it safe to drink.   First, filter the water through a piece of porous material (like a handkerchief or t-shirt) to remove suspended particles and debris. Then purify it.

Purification

Most open sources of water you find will require treatment to make it safe for drinking. Exceptions might be bubbling springs, rain water, condensation in a solar still, and dew that collects on surfaces in the morning. There are many options available for water treatment on the market, all with their own advantages and drawbacks.

Ultraviolet Light

This is the same technology that has been used in water bottling plants for many years, and it is very effective. It's fast and it destroys viruses, bacteria, and protozoa (like giardia). It is best to use UV units with clear water. You can also use a clean porous cloth for a filter, or you can purify your water twice with the UV unit to ensure complete destruction of harmful microbes.

Pumps

Most pump style filters eliminate over 99% of all waterborne bacteria and common parasites, such as giardia. Plus, the filter inserts are easily replaced or repaired and can filter significant quantities of water before being replaced (some up to 200 gallons). I've used one for years that weighs less than one pound and cost $60, plus it has a flow rate of just over one quart per minute.

PUMP-STYLE WATER FILTER/PURIFICATION SYSTEM (KATADYN)

Straws

You can't get much simpler than this: put the straw in the filter, stick the filter in a water source, and drink – it's that easy. I have carried this kind of item since I found it a few years ago. It fits in the palm of my hand and weighs a couple ounces. It will fit into the smallest daypack, fanny pack or survival kit.

Bottles

This system integrates a filter and a water bottle into one. I love the simplicity – just fill it up and drink through the nozzle. No pumping, no waiting. The model I have holds 28 ounces and is about 11" long. It can process approximately 28 gallons before I need to replace the filter (which eliminates bacteria, protozoa, and viruses). Better yet, it improves taste.

A WATER BOTTLE WITH BUILT-IN FILTRATION SYSTEM (KATADYN EXSTREAM)

Tablets

This is the essence of ultra-light – a
sheet of tablets weighs a couple
ounces. However, the water needs to
be clear and the tablets need time to
take effect. I pack these as a backup
and they are solid peace-of-mind
survival kit items. Iodine tablets also
work well – I relied on them for years
with no problems (you can find iodine
tablets in most Army Surplus stores).

Boiling

Boiling water for 10 minutes will kill
bacteria and make water suitable for
drinking (a full, rolling boil). Boiling will
also oxygenate the water, which can do
wonders for the taste.

Alternate Sources

Rain

Cups and water bottles are obvious collection
devices when the drops begin to fall, but if

you use any kind of waterproof material for your shelter, place a container under a corner and funnel the run-off into it – this will increase the collection significantly. If you don't have a container, try scraping a depression in the ground and lining it with a piece of plastic – you can create a substantial basin of water that will last long after the rain has passed.

Snow and Ice

Melting snow in a metal cup next to a fire is easy and productive (Note: ice will give you more bang for your buck because it's denser than snow). You can also fill a zip-lock baggie with snow and place it between the layers of your clothes, allowing your body heat to slowly melt it (make *sure* there are no holes in the bag!). One caution: resist the urge to eat snow and ice, as it requires energy for your body to melt them and it can lower your core temperature in the process.

If you don't have a metal vessel to melt snow or ice in, wrap a big snowball in a shirt, handkerchief, or other porous material. Hang it near your fire and put a catch device underneath. This is also advantageous of the snow has a lot of debris (pine needles, dirt, etc) in it as the material will act as a filter.

Dew

Although time consuming, mopping dew off grass and rocks (or your shelter, if it's plastic or nylon) with an absorbent piece of material can yield a healthy supply of water in the morning. Wring the water into your mouth as you work or squeeze it into a container for future use. If you are walking through tall grass in the morning (or after a rainfall), wrap your ankles with absorbent material and stop every 15 minutes to wring out the water.

Marshy Areas

Soft, spongy ground near cattails or mud flats is obviously damp, but what little water you may see on the surface is likely stagnant. Find solid ground next to the marsh and dig a hole until water begins to collect in the bottom. Allow the hole to fill with water and let any sediment settle – it might take some time. The earth will act as a filter and improve the taste, but purifying is still recommended. Lining the hole with grass will also help with filtration and taste.

Digging

Digging for water can be a fruitless effort unless you find the right spot. First, look for an area that is low-lying and lush. Then locate an area where the soil is damp or darker than the surrounding terrain - good places to check are the bottoms of steep ravines and undercut bends of dry creek beds. Given these conditions, I can't recall a situation where I haven't found water within the first 12" of digging (a flat rock or sturdy stick will help the digging go faster). Once water begins to seep into the hole, step back and give it some time. Sediment will settle in a few minutes. Then you can skim the clear water off the top with a cup or suck it up with a length of rubber tubing.

Notes

❈ Solar stills are often promoted as an effective way to collect water in arid environments. This involves digging a deep hole, placing a catch receptacle in the bottom, spreading a plastic sheet over the hole and sealing it, and waiting for the water to cook out of the soil (or whatever you put in the still) and condensing on the plastic to eventually drip into your catch device. I've found them to be inadequate. The amount of sweat you will lose building one was more than I recovered from the stills by a long shot. I've talked to a couple people that love them. They are very dependent on the moisture content of the soil and whatever you put in the hole. I'm not discounting them completely, but I prefer to seek other methods before undertaking this labor.

❧ In an arid environment, a transpiration bag or vegetation bag is often effective. Using a clear plastic trash bag, cover and enclose a bundle of branches containing green vegetation, somewhere that is exposed to sunlight for as much of the day as possible. Before sealing the bag, put a small rock in the bag to create a low spot where water will collect. As the sun cooks the vegetation, moisture will evaporate and condense on the plastic, trickling into the low spot. A vegetation bag is the same principle; however you fill the bag with green vegetation and set it in the sun. The water yielded will be greenish and might taste bad, but it is water.

Water Intake Requirements

Carl Weil has been teaching backcountry medicine for over thirty years and serves as the Medical Director for Wilderness Medical Outfitters. He offers the following equation for estimating the amount of water you should be consuming afield:

$$\frac{\text{Body Weight}}{35} = \text{Liters of water per day}$$

To convert to quarts, multiply the number of liters by 1.06

Tips

🌿 Remember to conserve your sweat, not your water. Work in the early morning or at night, when it is cooler.

🌿 Avoid the temptation to ration your water. The best storage device you have is your stomach.

🌿 Carrying a 2-foot long piece of hollow rubber surgical tubing will give you the ability to siphon water from small, bubbling springs or bowls in rock formations where water collects.

Chapter 7 - Food

In basic survival terms, the quest for food is a constant endeavor. The realistic duration of most modern survival episodes is usually a few days – not long enough for you to worry about "starving to death." But food provides energy and sustains health, and opportunities to supplement your diet – whether by carrying extra food or finding it in the woods – should never be overlooked. Remember that being hungry for a couple days might not be fun, but it will not kill you. Most important, don't eat a lot if you can't also drink a lot – your body needs the water for digestion, and large amounts of food without liquid will speed dehydration.

What You Can Take

Energy bars are a great idea. There are numerous types available, but look for high concentrations of carbohydrates. Carry a couple (you'll be glad if you get stuck) and don't eat them unless you need them -- they are your survival stash. Another excellent energy food is a bag of trail mix (chocolate candies, peanuts, and raisins). It's quick and nourishing, and it's easy to make your own. My best friend and I made it through a night on a big bag of trail mix and two canteens of water, and we didn't suffer a bit, considering we are both pretty big guys.

For minimal weight and high nutrition value, it's hard to beat freeze-dried meals. The downside is effort and preparation time (you must prepare boiling water and allow the meal to reconstitute). They require a little more room and some extra gear to use them, but they are worth it.

Military "Meals Ready to Eat" (MRE) rations are simple and effective, but comparatively heavy. The individual food components are packaged in a heavy foil pouch, and all the components are sealed together in a big plastic bag. I suggest cutting open the plastic bag and removing the individual foil-wrapped meal components (a normal ration pouch will include the main course, crackers, cracker topping, a cookie or other sweet, drink powder, condiments, and a few other odds and ends). This saves room and you can carry just the items you want. They can be eaten as-is (cold), heated next to a fire (the foil will hold up well), or you can use a MRE heater (a small plastic sleeve that, when water is added, will heat up a meal packet).

What You Can Find

When trying to find food sources in a survival situation, a good rule is to get more calories in return than you expend – this means maximum gain for minimal effort.

Plants

Plants are an advantageous wild food source because they are generally easy to find and require minimal effort to harvest. One word of caution: if you are not absolutely sure as to the edibility of a plant, avoid it. Every region of the country has particular plants that are good food sources. Local colleges or community centers sometimes offer classes on regional plant life that are very informative. It's a good idea to be familiar with edible plants that grow in your area. It would be impractical to try to list every edible plant you could encounter, but there are some universal rules about what NOT to eat, and that can be even more important.

What to Avoid

* Green, yellow, and white berries

* Mushrooms - As a general rule of safety and survival, avoid mushrooms altogether. They have little nutrition and even experts can get confused on the difference between safe and toxic mushrooms.

- Shiny leaves

- Umbrella-shaped flowers

- Milky sap

What to Look For

Dandelions

It's not hard to recognize this notorious lawn weed, found in just about any area where grasses grow. The flower (whether blooming or bud) and leaves are edible, raw or cooked – discard the stem.

Cattails

Found along stream, ponds, and marshy areas. The seed head, when green, can be eaten like corn on the cob and boiling first will help. Pull young shoots from the center of the stalk-like, green leaf clusters and eat them like a stick of celery.

Ferns

Ferns generally grow in shady areas with damp soil. The best part to eat is often referred to as a "fiddle head," which accurately describes the appearance of the tight-curling tips of fern shoots. These can be snapped off and collected in large quantities. They are best eaten after being boiled.

Cactus

In many western regions, various cactus plants cover the landscape. More common varieties are prickly pear and barrel cactus, which both have small fruit that grow on the tops during various parts of the season, ranging in color from green to purple and red. These fruit can be eaten raw or cooked. Prickly pear lobes can also be eaten, but it is best to scorch them first to remove the spines and then peel the outer layer of skin off.

Berries

Dark colored, preferably blue or black, and aggregate (small cells clumped together, like blackberries) are the safest choice for berries.

Insects

Insects can be found in great numbers and don't pose much of a challenge for harvest. They are also high in protein.

What to Avoid

- Bright colors

- Hairy bodies (like caterpillars and spiders)

- Possible disease carriers (such as ticks and mosquitoes)

- Stingers

What to Look For

Worms

Leach them in water if possible before eating, squeezing the body like a tube of toothpaste to remove grit. Eat them raw or cooked.

Grasshoppers

Personally, I prefer to remove the legs and wings before consuming. To avoid possible parasites, cook the bodies first (you can put them on a hot rock from the fire or even use the flame from a lighter).

Ants

Too small? Ask Air Force fighter pilot Scott O'Grady, who was shot down in 1995 over Bosnia. He ate ants (and plants) for six days until he was rescued. Avoid ants that have any red on them. Big carpenter ants can be found in rotten stumps and dead logs. Pinch the heads first to eliminate the mandibles.

Fish

The first time I had to fish for survival instead of recreation, I was doubtful. After years of fishing the Snake River in Idaho, a tiny two-foot wide trickle seemed hardly worth the effort. But an hour of crawling through logjams and thickets resulted in several small trout that filled my stomach. And over the years, I came up with a basic fishing kit that works well:

※ First, line wrapped around a small wooden dowel. This helps keep the line untangled, especially when unwinding it and it is easy to use this as a spool if you like to hand line. I usually cut a sapling or branch for a rod, but it is nice to have the option. I carry enough 6 pound test line to make several sapling rods, since I sometimes snag or otherwise lose my hook.

※ Next, a few lures and wet flies. This is important in a couple ways. If you are in a snowy environment, or you just can't find suitable live bait, you have effective attractor bait. The lures I use are small Colorado spinners – simple and effective. For wet flies, I carry 3 or 4 weighted attractor patterns such as Wooly Worms.

※ Last, small hooks and sinkers. I see a lot of commercial survival kits packed with enough fishing gear to reel in a Marlin. Reality has taught me that most situations are in small creeks or ponds, and a small hook can still catch a big fish. The opposite is a much harder proposition. The hooks are sizes 6, 8, and 10. The weights are BB size.

There are many ways you can improvise tools to catch fish, a few of which are very simple and require little more than creativity. First, just about any piece of wire can be fashioned into a hook, and whittling one from small "Y" branches or bones isn't very difficult. Safety pins make especially good improvised fishhooks as well.

My favorite improvised "hook" is actually a gorge, which is a small (about ¾" long) piece of wood, a little thicker than a toothpick, and sharpened on both ends. By scoring a small groove around the middle, you can attach a line and thread the gorge through a piece of bait.

When the fish pulls in the bait, the gorge will take hold on two sides and let you retrieve the fish. The length of the gorge is determined by the likely size of fish you are trying to catch. Again, smaller is usually better. Improvised fishing line can be fashioned from almost anything, but my favorite is the thin nylon core fibers from parachute cord (found in many sporting goods stores and military surplus outlets).

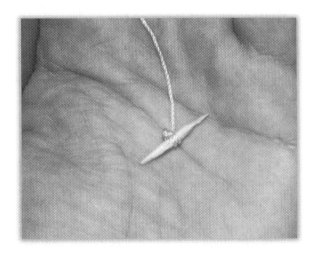

FISH GORGE ATTACHED TO NYLON INNER CORE STRAND FROM PARACHUTE CORD

Preparing Fish

Once caught, fish need to be cleaned by removing all the entrails and gills. This is best done by cutting up the belly from the anus to the "chin" and pulling everything out. Cut the stomach open to examine the contents – it can give you a good idea of what else they are eating and make your bait selection more effective in the future.

My favorite way to cook fish is wrapping them in aluminum foil and burying the package in the coals for about 15 minutes. Most commercial survival kits have foil in them, and it's never a bad idea to pack some. It is lightweight and takes up little room. When you open up the foil after the fish is cooked, you can pick the meat off the bones in big white flakes.

For cold water fish like trout, the skin is edible as is. For warm water fish like bass and bluegill, the scales should be removed from the skin first. This is easily done by scraping your knife blade on the skin (90 degrees to the surface of the skin) from tail to head on both sides.

Other cooking methods include skewering the fish on a green branch and roasting it over the flames of a fire, or setting it on a hot rock next to the fire and turning it over a few times as it broils.

Small Game

Small game is preferable to large game due to proliferation and effort required to harvest. There are many weapons and hunting implements that can be fashioned over time, such as slingshots, bows, traps, and so on, and they all work well in the hands of someone who is familiar with them. However, these can take a lot of time and finesse to construct and use. There are also many intricate snare trigger devices and deadfalls that can be made, but generally speaking, simple snares are better. There are fewer chances the trap will be accidentally triggered and they take less time to build and set – the more snares you can put out the better. To save time and energy, a simple snare can hunt for you while you are taking care of other needs. Wire works best, but thin cord can also get the job done.

How to Build a Simple Loop Snare

1. Use two or three feet of light wire (24 gauge copper or picture hanging wire is the best I've found)

2. Twist a small (1/2") fixed loop into on one end of the wire. Twist the loop once in the middle, making a figure eight. Fold the two lobes of the eight over each other, making a double loop.

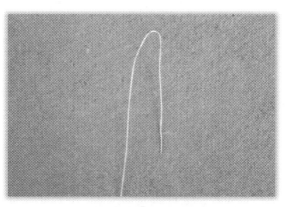

1

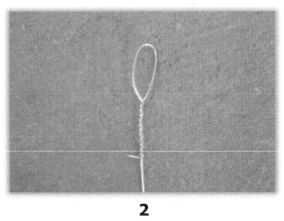

2

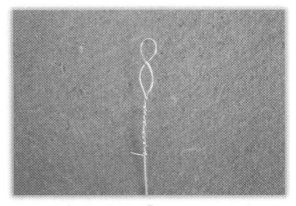

3

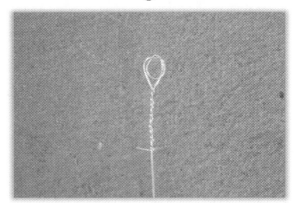

4

3. Thread the tail end of the wire through the double loop. Close and adjust the snare opening until it is round and the desired size (about 3 fingers wide for squirrels and 4 fingers wide for rabbits). The double loop will close on the snare wire when an animal pulls, causing the double loop to "lock" and not slip.

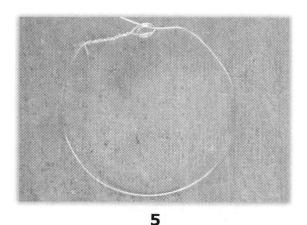

5

How to Set a Simple Loop Snare

1. Look for locations where the animal is "funneled" into a specific spot; i.e. the animal's head will have to pass through a certain space in order to move down a path. You can create your own funneling by pushing sticks into the dirt along a path

and bring them closer together to a pinch point, where your snare will be set.

2. You are also wise to place the snare at the entrance to well-used den or burrow (look for an absence of cob webs, fresh dirt, and smooth entrance path).

3. Fashion the noose to be slightly bigger than the intended quarry's head and attach the snare to a solid anchor (a root or stake works well).

4. Check them each morning and evening.

AN EXCELLENT LOCATION TO SET A SNARE

Preparing Small Game

Remove the entrails and skin from game animals before cooking and consuming. For small game like rabbits and squirrels, this can be done quickly and simply.

First, make a 1" cut in the hide in the middle of the back, right over the spine. Next, work the pointer and middle fingers of each hand into the cut and grasp the hide on either side of the incision. Now pull your hands apart, one toward the head and one toward the tail. This will strip the hide off the body and leave it attached at the feet, head, and tail. Sever these with a knife and then slit the body cavity open along the belly.

Remove the entrails and keep the heart, kidneys, and liver – they are edible. However, check the liver for white bumps or splotches; if present, this indicates tularemia and the internal organs should be discarded. The remaining parts are edible but should be cooked thoroughly.

For birds, you don't even need a knife to prepare them. Using your fingers, you can open the visceral cavity just below the breast bone by pulling at the skin. Remove the entrails. Pluck the feathers off and keep the skin because it has important fat and nutrients. Immersing the bird in water for a few minutes first will sometimes make this easier. You can scorch off any small feathers you miss.

Cooking methods are similar to what has been described above (roasting on a stick, frying on a rock, or wrapping in foil and burying in the coals). In addition, you can place the carcass directly on the coals of a fire and roast the meat. However, boiling is the preferred method if you have the means. This is the most beneficial in terms of nutrients and hydration (drink the broth after you've eaten the meat).

Chapter 8 - First Aid

The subject of backcountry first aid has comprised several books, and this chapter will not make you an expert. However, a central theme of wilderness first aid is to prevent common injuries from becoming major problems. These tips will help you get started and make sure you are prepared for unforeseen accidents that can complicate your outdoor experience.

Supplies

A well-equipped first aid kit should be a mandatory part of your gear. Chose items to fit your pack and your capabilities, but always include the basics: materials necessary to control bleeding, clean and package wounds, and take care of personal medical conditions. These basics might include:

- Personal medications
- Band-aids of various sizes
- Alcohol wipes

- Antibiotic ointment
- Tweezers
- Moleskin
- Assorted gauze pads
- Triangular bandage and safety pins
- Roll of medical tape
- Soft splint (optional)
- ACE wrap (optional)
- Petroleum jelly (optional)
- Cold pack (optional)

Common Injuries

A recent academic study[1] was conducted that evaluated types of injuries suffered by visitors to Yosemite National Park who were the subjects of Search and Rescue operations. The study covered a ten year period starting in the mid 90s and recorded 2,077 injuries. Some of the most common were:

---

[1] *Wilderness and Environmental Medicine:* Vol. 18, No. 2, pp. 111-116.

Fractures, Sprains, Dislocations	36.4%
Lacerations, Abrasions	11.3%
Dehydration, Hunger	8.3%
Hypothermia, Frostbite	4.6%

Of course, this is a general sample and took place in one particular area. However I believe it to be an accurate representation of what you should prepare for, at a minimum.

Blisters

Boots and socks should fit properly to ensure your feet are able to walk you out of the wilderness. Besides properly-fitting boots, a thin polypropylene sock under a thicker wool sock can also reduce friction and rubbing. But even properly fit boots and socks can lead to blisters during a heavy day of hiking. For this, moleskin can save your feet; a 3" X 4" square is indispensable and can be found in most drug stores. If you feel a "hot spot" develop on your foot, apply the moleskin immediately (cut it big enough to easily cover the hot spot) and check it each night in camp. Some people use a few strips of medical tape to do the same thing. Don't break any blisters that form, but if it does happen, apply antibiotic ointment and protect with a bandage (I tape on the bandage so it doesn't slip off while I'm hiking).

Incisions and Lacerations

According to Carl Weil, Medical Director for the Colorado-based Wilderness Medical Outfitters, direct pressure on an incision, combined with elevating the injured area above the heart (if possible), will stop 97% of all bleeding. "Irrigating the wound with sterile water will clean the wound and help prevent infection," he added. For this, he advises carrying a large syringe (minus the needle, of course) to direct a gentle but focused stream of water into the cut to remove dirt and debris. You can improvise by filling a plastic sandwich bag with water, poking a small hole in one corner, and squeezing to create a pressure stream. Then apply antibiotic ointment, bandage with a band-aid or gauze dressing, and protect it from contamination. If the incision is more than ½' wide, it's a good idea to pack it open using clean, moist gauze inside the cut, and dry dressings on top. Then, protect the injury from outside contamination. Check the wound often for signs of infection – redness, swelling, or pus build up. If this happens, cleanse the wound thoroughly and re-bandage with clean dressings. You can improvise gauze strips by cutting up a clean t-shirt or other similar item.

Frostbite

The most important way to treat frostbite is prevention. Don't tolerate painfully cold or numb fingers or toes – immediately start to re-warm the effected digits. You can do this with skin-to-skin contact or using the "windmill" for your fingers. This involves you swinging your arms in big circles, which forces blood into your fingers and generates body heat. Also, maintain good circulation - don't wear constricting clothing, don't lace your boots too tight, and avoid ingesting alcohol and tobacco in cold weather. Minor or early frostbite will give your skin a pale or even gray appearance. It can be numb or aching. You can warm the affected part with skin-to-skin contact or, if you have the means, use Weil's suggestion:

* Be gentle with the affected body part and don't rub it to re-warm – this can cause further tissue damage

* Immerse the affected body part in warm water (104-106 degrees) and wrap in loose, warm bandages (if the frostbite is severe, meaning the affected body part is grayish-blue and wood-like, do not attempt to re-warm under any circumstances and proceed directly to a medical facility)

* Ensure there is no chance of the affected body part freezing again, as this can turn a minor injury into a crippling one. Note: Avoid re-warming frostbitten feet in the field – the re-warming process will be painful and may limit your ability to walk out of the woods.

Hypothermia

Hypothermia (lowering of the body's core temperature below 97 degrees) can cause poor decision-making and loss of coordination. Untreated, it can lead to coma and death. Most people attribute it to arctic-like conditions however it is more common in cool, rainy weather.

If you find yourself shivering uncontrollably (the first sign of hypothermia), you need to take action *now*; don't try to "push through it." Hypothermia is a medical condition. I doubt you would ignore a bleeding injury, so likewise you should not ignore the fact that you are so cold you can't stop shivering. Even though this is the early stage of hypothermia, toughing it out won't help. Drinking warm liquids won't stop it, either, according to Gates Richards, the Director of Wilderness Emergency Medical Technician training at the Wilderness Medical Institute. "Staying hydrated is important, and warm liquids are more appealing in cold weather," Gates stated, "but the warmth of your 16 ounces of hot chocolate has no measureable effect on your core temperature." However, sugary liquid will add calories to your system and get metabolism going, and that can increase body temperature slightly. So will foods that are high in carbohydrates. But the best treatment is to stop, build a fire, and warm up. Protect yourself from the weather, dry any wet clothes, and get into a sleeping bag if possible.

Venomous Snake Bites

"There are more than 8,000 snakebites every year," Weil said, "but only about eight of those will be fatal." The three don'ts: don't cut an "X" over each fang hole (as once prescribed), don't use a tourniquet, and don't pack the wound with ice. The old guidance to cut X's over the fang holes and suck out the venom with your mouth is no longer accepted. In fact, it is absolutely discouraged. Cutting just creates another injury to deal with. There are tools to help remove venom, such as the Sawyer Extractor, but it needs to be applied within 3 minutes of the bite to be most effective. Avoid using tourniquets or applying ice – the ice can further damage the tissue and does not slow the absorption of venom. The most important thing to do is stay calm. Then, clean the bite site and immobilize the extremity affected. "Evacuate the patient, ideally without making them walk," Gates added. This will slow the spread of venom in the bloodstream.

Joint and Skeletal Injuries

These injuries need to be treated with great caution – diagnosis of fractures, sprains, dislocations, and similar injuries can be difficult if not impossible without the aid of an X-ray machine. Gates suggests evaluating the damage based on the victim's ability to manipulate the joint or bear weight on the injured extremity. If the person twisted their ankle painfully, but can still bear weight on it and walk, tape the joint for support. If the person cannot stand on an injured leg, take a more careful approach and treat for the worst-case. "Create a well-padded splint that immobilizes the injury," Gates said. "This usually means immobilizing the bones or joints above and below the injury site."

Learning More

Red Cross offices and community colleges often teach first aid classes, and a call to the local Search and Rescue unit might turn up some wilderness-specific medical training in your area. Also see Chapter 14 for additional reading and Chapter 15 for medical training.

Chapter 9 –Rescue

Survival skills are important if you become lost or stranded, but it is more preferable to end the situation before having to use them. I've heard many people talk about survival situations by saying something like: "I'll just sit and wait for them to find me." Good idea, but why not make it easier for "them" – the Search and Rescue heroes working to rescue you. In fact, the more conscious you are of opportunities to build or use signals, the shorter your survival situation will be. Here are a few tools and techniques that will tell rescuers where to find you.

Whistle

Inexpensive, small, and effective, a whistle is a must for your survival gear. A few blasts can quickly reunite lost partners or aid searchers on the ground. A whistle will outlast your vocal cords, and it takes less energy (and emotion) than yelling.

The New Mexico Department of Game and Fish gives every graduate of Hunter Education a 5-in-1 survival tool that has a whistle built into it. I hear a lot of people joke about scaring away animals or creating a commotion by blowing a whistle if they get turned around. My response: so what. Better to avoid getting stuck in the woods.

5-IN-1 TOOL

Example: One of my friends asked me to build him a survival kit and explain what to do if he got lost – sort of a crash-course in survival. I was going hunting with him later in the fall as a "guide" to help with spotting and packing. I spent a few hours talking with him and stressing the importance of staying put and signaling me if he got lost. Sure enough, we got separated later that fall as we walked through some brushy canyons. We were about a mile from camp and I climbed to the top of a rocky formation to see if I could spot him walking back to camp. As I stood there looking through my binoculars, I heard the unmistakable sound of a signal whistle. It took me just a few minutes to reunite with my friend and we continued on without a hitch. It can be that simple, but that effective. Blowing your whistle in a series of three quick blasts (the universal distress code) will help draw attention even faster.

Mirror

Flashes of sunlight from a signal mirror can be seen from several miles away. They range in size, but a bigger mirror will create a bigger flash. I like the military-style signal mirror, which measures about 2" X 3" and has a helpful sighting hole in the middle of it. If you don't have a sighting hole, try the following:

1. Hold the mirror in your strong hand and place it directly under your sighting eye

2. Stretch out your other arm and turn your palm toward your face, fingers extended

3. Flash the light on the fingertips of your outstretched hand and create a "V" with your index and middle fingers

4. Put your target in the "V" and rock the mirror back and forth lightly – this creates "flashes" which will draw attention and communicate an immediate message of distress. Don't stop flashing until the target is out of sight.

AIMING A SIGNAL MIRROR

Ground-to-Air

Ground-to-air signals are constant beacons to assist aerial search parties. Once constructed, they can take care of signaling while you busy yourself meeting other survival needs. To make your effort worthwhile, follow these guidelines:

❧ Select a site that is elevated and open

❧ Use material that will contrast with the environment (such as dead logs on green grass, light-colored rocks on dark soil, overturned dirt in a field of wildflowers, or exposed ground in the snow)

❧ Create a signal that has straight lines and sharp angles such as an "X" or "V" – these are universal distress codes – and remember that bigger is better.

❧ Heavyweight "sportsman" space blankets – silver on one side and colored on the other – can be found in colors such as blaze orange and bright red. Laying the colored-side up in a meadow or snowfield makes a great signal, or you can build a shelter with it (colored-side facing the sky) and let it pull double duty.

Cellular Phones and Emergency Radios

According to James Newberry, Search and Rescue Resource Officer for the State of New Mexico, advances in technology have cut down search times and increased the number of successful rescues. "If someone is talking with our searchers [on a cellular phone] and describing their location," says Newberry, "we can get to them much faster."

Handheld two-way radios with an emergency channel are also helpful, but they can be limited by shorter transmission range and terrain obstacles. When using any electronic communications device, seek out the highest point possible and keep trying, even if your first attempts seem to be unsuccessful. I once observed the initiation of a search and rescue operation when a passing truck driver picked up the distress call from a lost hiker some ten miles away.

Flares

Smoke

If aircraft are in the area, a smoke flare can pinpoint your location to them. However, smoke flares are single-use signals; once it ignites and burns, it's done (unless you carry several, which can be expensive and heavy). Ignite the flare as the aircraft approaches (rather than after it passes) so the smoke has time to billow out and create a big, visible cloud.

Illumination

Obviously intended for low-light conditions, illumination flares are great in open areas such as snowfields and bodies of water; they are visible for long distances and come in several colors that stand out well. Avoid injury when using these by thoroughly understanding how it works and wearing gloves when you ignite it.

Projectile

Projectile flares are launched several hundred feet into the air via a handheld trigger and burn as they descend. Some utilize small rockets about the size of a rifle cartridge; others look like road flares and are single-shot signals. They are effective for marking your location if you hunt in thick timber and steep canyons as they can elevate your signal and make it visible over a wide area. Carry several spare rockets and know how to use them correctly.

Smoke Generator

Your campfire is a signal by itself, but you can make it even better – here's how: Stack a heap of green pine boughs near your fire (the more boughs, the better). If a plane or helicopter passes over (or you hear one in the area), pile them onto your fire (it needs to be a strong, hot fire) and a column of white smoke will rise into the atmosphere like a smokestack. Remember that clarity of the atmosphere will affect the visibility of your smoke. If possible, avoid dense overhead foliage, as it will potentially cause the smoke to dissipate.

Chapter 10 – Positive Attitude

By now you have a good idea of what tools and techniques it takes to survive in the wilderness. But there is one aspect of survival that isn't as easy to learn. You can't buy it at a store, it isn't found in the woods, but it is perhaps the most important tool you can have for survival: positive attitude.

So what is it, and how do you get it? There are a lot of ways I could explain what it is, but the basic principles are 1) don't give up, and 2) refuse to feel helpless. Positive attitude is the drive that tells you to never quit trying, even if your first attempts are not successful. It's the understanding that there are people who very much want you to return home safely. It's the realization that there are people looking for you and determined to rescue you. It's the feeling that you can overcome obstacles and take care of yourself.

Everyone is wired differently, so telling you how to "get" an emotion is impossible. But, I can tell you what will help develop it, no matter who you are.

Confidence

I've discussed this in several places thus far, and confidence is born out of preparation.

Determination

You will not give up and you will overcome your problems. You can do it.

Faith

In your family, in the searchers, in religion, in yourself - whatever motivates you to believe.

My dad always told me to keep trying, no matter what. Never quit. Well, one training trip I had to literally spoon-feed this philosophy to a student from New York who had never been in the woods. He was petrified. He came up to me the first day and said he wanted to quit. This guy had to graduate from the training course to get his certification as a flight crewmember, a highly sought after job. But he was willing to throw it away without a second thought because he was so intimidated by the wilderness. I tried to tell him that it would be OK, and he could do it if he just stuck it out. It didn't work. He wanted to quit. So I played a trick on him. I told him he couldn't quit because we had no way to get him out of the woods, and he would have to wait until tomorrow. The next day, he approached me again. I told him that my supervisor was at the next checkpoint so he might as well hike there to talk with him. When we got to the checkpoint, of course my supervisor wasn't there, so I told him he might was well get some sleep and we'd take care of it tomorrow. I went through this for a week. On the last day, when he approached me yet again, I told him, "Why quit now, you're done." He looked at me quizzically and then started crying. He showed himself he could do it, even when he tried not to. But it took a different approach: deal with things one day at a time. Do what it takes to get to the next day, make it your goal. Don't look at the totality of the situation...that might be a little heavy. Look at it in manageable pieces. If one day seems like too much, get through one hour at a time, or even one minute at a time. Break the situation down into pieces that you can focus on and deal with more easily. As the old saying goes: *How do you eat an elephant? One bite at a time...*

I remember another situation that illustrates how positive attitude can make or break a survival situation. I was leading a group of students during a winter training trip, and one particular student wasn't having fun. He was out of shape and generally a grump. However, he was higher ranking than I was and didn't like a junior person telling him what to do. One afternoon we were a couple miles from camp and were heading back from a long day of hiking. It was cold, but not miserable. We were walking downhill, which was a good thing, and the weather was calm. The group was fatigued and everyone was pretty quiet. We stopped for a drink of water and this student plopped down on a stump and sulked. When it was time to resume our trek, I mustered everyone to their feet but he didn't budge. I walked over and asked him if he was OK. He just glared at me.

"I think we should stay here," he said, "We are tired of hiking and my back hurts."

"Let's go." I told him, "We can rest at camp."

"I'm not going ANYWHERE!" He yelled at me, on the verge of tears. It was like dealing with a small child.

Finally, I told him, "Sitting here isn't going to solve any of your problems. If you want to stay here, fine, but we are leaving." I turned and walked down the trail with the group. And the student fell in at the rear, reluctantly. A week later, after we were back in civilization, he apologized.

"I don't know what my problem was," he said.

I did. He had a negative attitude that led him to believe he had more problems than solutions. That he could not cope. That giving up was his only option. If he had given up, he'd still be there on the stump, a skeleton. One of my favorite sayings is a line from the movie Shawshank Redemption, where Morgan Freeman's character says, "Either get busy living, or get busy dying." This is the essence of keeping a positive attitude: Get busy living.

Chapter 11 – Vehicles

You put a lot of thought into the gear you're going to carry into the wilderness, but do you think about the gear you should have in your vehicle? For example, the New Mexico Department of Public Safety logged 40 Search and Rescue missions between 2002 and 2004 to look for people stranded in vehicles[2]. If you get stuck in transit to your trailhead or camping spot, especially in a remote area, you will still have the same survival needs: warmth, shelter, water, and so on. These require the same kinds of items you might put in a pack: firestarter (and backup), signal mirror, whistle, knife, tarp or poncho, food, water, rope, sleeping bag or wool blanket, warm clothes, and even an axe. But there are also big differences.

Getting a vehicle "unstuck" can require unique tools, like a jack, winch, shovel, and towrope or chain. Depending on the kind of vehicle you drive, the engine can require some pretty specific tools to make even minor adjustments – be sure to know what you need and how to use it. Road flares or reflective cones are important safety

---

[2] New Mexico Search and Rescue Annual Statistics 2002-2004, www.dps.nm.org/lawenforcement/searchrescue/statistics

considerations and will help passing motorists see your distress, and a CB or emergency channel radio transmitter can bring a sticky situation to a close much faster. If you have the means to communicate, a GPS will enable you to give searchers your exact location, rather than trying to describe the area around you or how you got there.

What to Take

I keep a large plastic trunk packed and ready so that I can throw it in the back of my truck when I leave for a trip. It gives me the tools I need to deal with just about anything on the road. It contains the following:

- Tow rope

- Tool kit

- Jumper cables

- Flashlight and extra batteries (replace batteries periodically)

- First aid kit (check expiration dates annually)

- Nylon tarp

- Warm clothes (wool shirt, hat, and rain suit)

- Firestarters, matches, lighter, metal match

- Mirror and whistle

- Knife

- Axe and small shovel

- Orange nylon signal panel

- Rope

In addition to this kit, I carry a cellular telephone and an atlas of topographical maps. Other items to consider carrying are:

- Road flares and/or reflective cones

- GPS

- Tire chains

Before you go, especially on a long trip, inspect the mechanical condition of your vehicle and ensure everything is in proper working order. This includes the fluid levels, battery, heater, tire pressure, and spare.

What to Do

Let's say you slide off the road somewhere and can't recover the vehicle. First and foremost, don't panic. Stay with your vehicle. It is a signal, a refuge, and a source of survival tools. Unless your rig takes a tumble off the mountain (in which case you will have some additional issues to deal with), it will be on or near a human line of passage, which greatly increases your odds of being seen or discovered. One exception to the rule of staying with your vehicle would be if you know exactly where you are and conditions are safe for you to travel for help.

Otherwise, consider your vehicle a ready-made shelter (unless it was damaged in some way and would not be safe). You can start your engine periodically and run the heater for warmth. Keep running time to no more than ten minutes each hour, and less is preferable. Ensure you clear away any blockages around the exhaust pipe and roll a window down to avoid carbon monoxide build-up. While the engine is running, try to find a radio channel for storm updates or news about rescue efforts. Don't sleep with the engine running (instead, bundle up in warm clothes and sleeping bags or blankets), and keep your feet off the floorboards where cold air collects. If you are in a large vehicle, partition off the front compartment (where you are) to conserve heat. If you are without blankets or a sleeping bag, the foam padding in the other seats can be removed and used for insulation (it might be ugly and cost money to repair, but your life is worth it).

If you are in an area where thick trees are beside the road, you have the opportunity to get a fire going nearby – it's warmth and a signal. If you are stranded near a large field, stomp out a ground-to-air SOS or other signal. Be flexible and look at your options.

There are also several signals associated with your vehicle. There are multiple mirrors that can be removed and used for flashing at passing aircraft - Compact Disks from your music player are especially good for this use. Tie something bright and colorful (such as trail marking tape or an orange vest) to the vehicle's antenna to serve as a signal flag, and keep the top surfaces clear of snow so they'll stand out better against the environment. The horn can signal ground search parties, but use it sparingly to avoid drawing down the battery.

Chapter 12 – Challenging Conditions

This book covers the basics of survival and focuses on the simplest, fastest way to meet your needs. There are many variables that can affect a survival situation, and it would take volumes to cover them all. One point you must remember is that the basics of survival will always be the same; the fire triangle is does not change in an arctic environment versus a desert; your body will need water in the jungle or in the woods behind your house, and so on. But how you accomplish these needs can require creativity and adaptation from time to time.

This chapter will address a few situations that could be described as "outside the norm" but a fairly real possibility if you spend enough time in the woods. It's best to think about them now and get a few ideas before you have to face them.

A Dunk in the Creek

It can be a funny situation, a clumsy gaffe or slip (the most common occurrence with me), but it should not be ignored. I'm not talking about getting your feet wet or even stumbling onto your knees in some water (those situations still need to be dealt with, but they aren't as threatening); I'm talking about submersion with your clothes getting soaked.

It will probably leave you gasping no matter what time of year it happens; creek water is cold. This can cause you to panic a bit. First, get out of the water, calm down, and resist the urge to run in the direction you need to go (a common reaction). Take a few deep breaths and tell yourself that you aren't going anywhere: you need to stay right here and deal with this. Some folks say it is acceptable to "walk dry" your wet clothes (letting your body heat help with the drying process). I disagree. That might be okay if your pant legs get wet, but not if you are soaked. Wet clothing conducts heat away from your body and the insulation value of garments is degraded if not ruined. Don't take risks; just sit down, build a fire, and dry out.

If two people are hiking together and this happens to one, the other needs to immediately begin making preparations for a fire. If you are alone, it is up to you and your gear. Hopefully you protected your survival kit well enough and you have dry tinder and ignition sources. Review the principles of building a good fire (Chapter 5). Don't skip steps or take shortcuts; you need this fire. If it is warm, sunny weather, the person who is wet will probably not be all that uncomfortable while the fire is being built. If the weather is windy and cold, this takes on a whole different flavor. Regardless, hypothermia is a very real possibility and the faster you can get a fire built, the better (see chapter 13 for Practical Exercises to sharpen your skills). Once the fire is established, take your time and make sure you are warm and dry before setting out again.

Blizzard

Day hiking is popular in northern New Mexico. There are many big peaks with good trail systems that enable people to get from their vehicle to the top of a mountain and back in a day. Some of these peaks are 12,000 feet or higher. I've been on a few of these hikes, up to 10,000 feet or so, and run into some of the "hardcore" hikers who were passing me. They tend to have on very light and minimal clothing, carry several water bottles, and maybe a fanny pack or small daypack.

They want a light load and plan to travel fast (some even jog).

I talked with a few of these hikers at trailheads and every one of them has dealt with high country snow storms in the summer months. Some seem to be ready for such an eventuality but others don't seem to worry much. From my own experience, the snow will hit hard and arrive in a rush. They sky can go from clear to cloudy to blizzard in a shockingly short period of time, almost like someone threw a switch. If you spend any significant amount of time in the high country, it's bound to happen. Resist the urge to try to outrun the storm. Switch gears and go through what you might call an "immediate action drill."

First, find some sort of physical barrier to the wind. It can be anything: trees, rocks, even a quick poncho shelter you throw up. I try to do this in a covered area, such as a stand of timber or in a saddle below the peak of a hill. In an area where there are very few terrain features, it might even be necessary to pile up rocks or dig out a trench behind a fallen tree or log. If wind isn't a major factor, move to the next concern: get out of the falling snow. My favorite quick shelter, as I mentioned in Chapter 4, is a tree well – they work fantastic in snow storms. You can easily improve on them by lining the bottom with a thick layer of boughs as an insulation barrier, and incorporating a shelter piece into the branches as an additional shield from snow and wind.

Next, I protect my clothing and my body by adding an "outer shell" layer (see Chapter 1 regarding clothing). If you are out of the wind and precipitation, and your clothing is adequate, you can ride out some pretty bad storms at this point.

Last, I make preparations for a fire. If I'm using a tree well, I will not be lighting a fire under the snow-laden branches, but I do have an abundance of dry fuel ready to go. The snow will eventually stop and I can dig out an area in front of the shelter to strike flames and warm up. I also like to look for protected areas around the rocky outcroppings often found just below a ridgeline. If I can find a wide space between two rocks that offers a wind break, a fire does wonders because the heat is reflected on two sides. One year in Washington a friend and I sat out an intense snowstorm this way for the better part of an afternoon.

If you are in an area with a layer of packed snow already underfoot, an easy shelter to use for a night is a snow trench. Dig a rectangular trench about 3 feet deep and slightly bigger than the dimensions of your body. Cover the "floor" with pine boughs. Use thick branches or poles to bridge across the trench, tightly spaced, and cover this with more boughs. Leave a small opening to crawl in and close it from the inside with more branches and boughs. It won't be roomy, but it will get you out of the weather and give you a quick shelter.

Extreme Heat

Another common environmental challenge I encounter in the southwest is high temperatures. The key to avoiding problems during these kinds of conditions is not falling behind the power curve; don't overexert in the heat or get dehydrated in the first place. These factors can complicate your situation and then survival really gets interesting. It is also one of my personal challenges; I dehydrate quickly and have to constantly remind myself to drink water. The climate in my area is very dry, so sweat evaporates almost immediately. It can make you feel like you aren't sweating so the urge to drink constantly is sometimes diminished. Conversely, in very humid environments, I am always covered in sweat and feel like I'm melting, so I'm always drinking. Pace your activities to avoid exhaustion, wear sun protection (wide brimmed hat, sun glasses, loose-fitting clothing made of light, porous materials, etc), and rest often.

If you do get stuck in the wilds, either because of or during extreme heat conditions, build a shelter that provides plenty of overhead shade and allows air to circulate. For instance, instead of making a lean-to with the back edge pulled tight to the ground, use long stakes to allow a foot or so of room between the ground and the bottom of the material. If you can construct your shelter in an area that will take advantage of additional shade created by surrounding trees or structures you will be even better off.

In areas where you might not have many trees or other structures to help with shelter, try this: Dig a shallow depression twice the width and slightly longer than your body; try to get it a foot or two deep (if you can find a naturally-occurring depression of some sort it will save a lot of time and sweat). Pile a few rocks (big and flat, if possible) at the four corners of the depression. Stretch your shelter piece across the four "pillars" and weight it down with a few more rocks. It will get you out of the sun and allow air circulation.

Water will become a top priority and you should be constantly thinking of ways to collect it as well as preserve it. Avoid eating large quantities of food if you do not have water and restrict work to hours of dawn, dusk, and darkness.

Lightning

My buddy and I were archery hunting in eastern Washington one fall. We concentrated our efforts in a rocky valley that was loosely timbered with big ponderosa pines. We'd seen plenty of deer and were content to stay right there for a few days. One evening without much warning, the wind picked up and a thunderstorm rolled into the area. We hunkered in a thick grove of fir trees at the bottom of a nearby draw and quickly set up a lean-to. We huddled in the setting darkness as the sky lit up with bolt after bolt of lightning. I silently hoped that the arcing electricity would find the surrounding bluffs more attractive than the place we'd bedded down. The wind howled and pushed trees back and forth as thunder boomed so loud it seemed to shake the ground. The storm lasted almost an hour, and it was a humbling example of nature's power. We laughed off our jittery nerves, but lightening is no joke and nothing to be taken lightly.

Be Aware

🌩 Each year, about 400 people are struck, directly or indirectly, by lightning while they are participating in outdoor activities. The statistics differ slightly, but an estimated 100 people subsequently die as a result (that's more than tornadoes, and when it comes to storms and bad weather, only floods kill more people). Just this year, a man was struck and killed by lightening near where I live while walking across a parking lot next to a soccer field.

🐾 About 10% of lightning strikes occur with blue skies above (lighting can travel "sideways" through the atmosphere), and lightning can strike well ahead of rain. Also remember that all thunderstorms produce lightning. So if you see storm clouds approaching or hear thunder in the distance, don't wait to see lightning to know it's there – seek protection immediately.

🐾 Light travels through the atmosphere faster than sound. If you see lighting and hear thunder simultaneously, the lightning is striking in your immediate vicinity. You need to take protective measures at once.

🐾 Lightning is created when positively and negatively charged particles in the atmosphere and on the earth create an electrical current. Some survivors of lightning strikes have described a tingling feeling on their skin and their hair standing on end just prior to the strike – a result of the charged particles traveling over their body. If you experience this feeling, immediately take protective actions (seek shelter, crouch down, etc)

🌑 Outdoors is the most dangerous place to be during a thunderstorm. If you get caught outside, stay far away from tall trees and metal structures (lighting can strike nearby objects and jump or arc to another object). If possible, seek shelter in a hard-topped vehicle or indoors. Remain there until well after the storm ends.

🌑 Avoid bodies of water completely. They are great conductors of electricity, and the charge from a strike can travel across the water, away from the point of impact.

🌑 Don't hold onto large metal objects during a storm, or if you are wearing them (such as an external pack frame), take it off.

🌑 The heat generated from the flash can reach 50,000 degrees Fahrenheit, which can (and does) start forest fires.

What to Do

High Country

Weather can move quickly in the mountains. Be aware of changing conditions and stay off bald peaks and open ridges at the first hint of dark clouds. I learned this lesson the hard way one sunny fall afternoon in southern Colorado. I'd stopped to rest during a long hike up a rocky ridge above timberline when a dark cloud formation blocked out the sun. I sat drinking water until big raindrops began to fall. I was pulling on my Gore-tex jacket when the first lightning strike happened. It was close enough that the flash and the thunder were simultaneous, and I realized that I had become the tallest point on the ridge. I scurried down the steep slopes as fast as I could while several more strikes rattled my nerves.

Open Areas

Avoid single trees or isolated structures. Seek cover in a ravine or gully if possible. Place insulating material, like a sleeping pad or jacket, between you and the ground and crouch on it.

Timber

Take cover in a low-lying area and among smaller saplings. Don't use single trees of groups of tall trees for protection.

First Aid

Contrary to popular myth, people struck by lightning are not "charged" and can be safely touched immediately afterward. Common effects of lightning strikes are cardiopulmonary arrest (a lack of breathing and heartbeat), burns, unconsciousness, deafness from ruptured eardrums, and traumatic injuries such as fractures and dislocations. It's important to react quickly and provide immediate attention. First, check for airway, breathing, and pulse. If necessary, initiate Cardiopulmonary Resuscitation (CPR). Second, stabilize and splint any fractures or dislocations. Third, stabilize the spine if necessary, especially if the person fell or was thrown a distance. Next, look for and treat any burns – especially in areas where metal was in contact with the skin (such as jewelry and zippers). Assuming here that you are in the wilds, call 911 as soon as possible as you evacuate the patient to the nearest medical facility. If you have the ability to do so when the strike occurs, call immediately.

Chapter 13 – Practical Exercises

Hopefully your head is now full of survival tips and techniques that will help you if you ever get stuck in the wilderness. The most effective way to refine your gear, decide what techniques you like or don't like, and figure out what your weak points are is to practice these skills before your life depends on it (and then practice some more). Survival kits are designed to be a tool you use, not something you create and then forget about. You will need to replace some items and sharpen blades, but there is no way to be more intimately familiar with what your kit is capable of doing than to test it.

The following are simple exercises to allow you to practice what you've been reading. Some you can do in the back yard, some on a hike, and some during your next campout. Try them, and then come up with your own tests as your skills improve. Whatever you do, make it fun.

Exercise #1 – Build a Fire

Sounds easy, doesn't it? There's no time limit on this, so don't cheat! Break your fuel into three stages and prepare your site properly. Use the items in your survival kit to get the flames going. Is your tinder easy to light, or does it take work? How long does the tinder burn? Do you need more matches? All these questions should be answered as you go, and be sure to make any useful adjustments to your kit. Replace items that don't work well or are difficult to use. The next time you try it, time yourself without rushing. Get an idea of how long it will take you. The more you practice, the faster you will be.

Exercise #2 – Fire in the Rain

Once you've built a few fires and feel comfortable with the contents of your survival kit, it's time to step it up a notch. The next time you are hiking or camping and it starts to rain, test your abilities by building a fire with what you have in your survival kit. NOTE: It is best to do this with a "base camp" nearby as a safety net. I've done this exercise with my friends 20 feet from a pop-up trailer, and it doesn't make it any easier. Put yourself in role and consider that, in a similar situation, you would really need a fire and the current conditions would make your success important. So be diligent about the fuel you collect and the site where you choose to build it. Now we can see if your tinder, matches, lighter, etc. are really up to the test; you might decide that something isn't. You can upgrade or replace it when you get back home.

Exercise #3 – Three Fires

The theory behind having the resources to build three fires is that this will help guarantee your being able to get the job done despite possible setbacks. Well, let's try it. When I was doing this kind of drill in training, the instructor used a canteen of water to douse each fire I got started, eliminating the possibility of cheating. What it really did was mimic the extreme circumstances that can happen if a load of snow lands on your fire. Plus, it is stressful. You don't necessarily have to take it to that length, but be honest with yourself. This exercise will show you whether you really have enough in your kit to do the job, and whether you need more practice starting fires.

Exercise #4 – Natural Tinder

The next time you are walking in the woods, gather as many natural types of tinder as you can find. Remember, if it looks like tinder, it will likely work (use the cotton ball principle – fluffy and dry). When you get back to camp or your house, try lighting them and see how they ignite and burn. This exercise will not only help familiarize you with the type of tinder available in your area, but also help you learn to look for the qualities of good tinder.

Exercise #5 – Five-Minute Fire

This is the graduation exercise for your fire-building practice. You can time yourself. Or, if you really want to make it challenging, have someone with you pick a random time along a walk in the woods (where legal) and tell you "Go!" Then, see if you can get a fire going in five minutes. Use whatever you have and whatever you can find.

This should be a sustainable fire, something that will stay lit and eat fuel as you put it on. "Knee-high" flames are the standard you want to achieve before saying "done!"

Exercise #6 – "What If" Game

Anytime you stop to rest during a hike, ask yourself, "What would I do it I had to survive right here, right now?" Look around and pick out likely shelter sites, your best source of dry firewood, a possible spot to set a snare, any hints in the environment itself as to what you can do to help sustain your life. This is sometimes referred to as developing "survival eyes." Here's an example: In the introduction, I wrote about the time my best friend and I got stranded in some rocky cliffs in Idaho. We hiked through a flat, sheltered saddle as we were scouting around that day, and I remembered thinking that it was the only ideal place I'd seen for setting up a good shelter. It was just a passing thought. But when we got stuck, I immediately remembered that spot and headed straight for it. It took about 10 minutes to get there, hiking back up a steep hillside, but it was a wise move. We were safe and protected for the night, and we had the resources we needed.

Exercise #7 - Tarp Shelter

This is a basic lab for applying what you read about building shelters and making it happen. It can be a tarp you buy at a hardware store, a large plastic sheet, a military poncho, you name it. Build a shelter with it. Make it big enough for you and your gear.

Just build it and have fun doing it. If you really want to have a good time, sleep out in it for a night, better yet, sleep out in it if it is raining or snowing. Nature has a way of revealing design flaws in the most direct way. Again, it is best to have a safety net close by the first time you do this. As your skills develop, make a shelter using only what you have in your kit. This exercise will let you see what you can realistically do with what you have.

Exercise #8 – Natural Shelter

The basic principles of a shelter – large enough for you and your gear, insulated appropriately, constructed with durability and safety in mind – all apply. Take some time to find the right spot. Then, come up with a plan before you start building. A well-insulated natural shelter will keep you warm through the night. Take all the time you want. Then, if you want to test your creation, sleep in it for a night and critique yourself. Be conscious of any local regulations regarding the use of green boughs or constructing a shelter.

Exercise #9 – Signal Mirror

You can do this anywhere, and it is really fun. I suggest you use a variety of reflective surfaces – CDs, mirrors, watch faces, knife blades – and see how easy or difficult it is to aim a flash at a specific object. NOTE: DO NOT FLASH AIRCRAFT; they will report it. Considering that a plane or helicopter can be several hundred to several thousand feet away when you are signaling at it, this exercise will show you how much you have to work at getting the right angles and aiming methods. At a minimum, use whatever mirror you pack in your kit. Some models with aiming holes will be easier to use than others. Here's the fun part: have a friend stand at the end of the street and try to flash him with the mirror. You want a significant separation because you can accidentally cheat by seeing where the flash is hitting and direct it to his/her face without aiming. Make sure your friend has sunglasses on – this way you can practice more!

Exercise #10 – Spend the Night

This is the final test. Take your survival kit – and I really would suggest you have a safety net when you do this – and prepare a camp for the night. Maybe stay for two nights to get a real taste of what you can do. Don't cheat, but if you feel like it's not working, retreat to your safety net. You do not want to create a situation ripe for hypothermia or injury just trying to be tough.

Here's an example of how this really works. During training many years ago, we were required to have a personal survival kit with us at all times. I kept a small metal Band-Aid can filled with survival items in my pocket, and many other students had similar kits. During one trip in December, a student in my class got up in the middle of the night to visit the restroom for an extended visit. He walked far enough away to preserve sanitation in the camp. When he finished, he walked back toward the camp but could not find it. He wandered in circles for an hour in the darkness, too embarrassed to whistle for help, and finally got tired enough to do something about it. He laid a huge bed of pine boughs down and fed a big fire all night, waking at fist dawn to see that he was within 50 yards of his shelter. This was his reality check that the survival kit he carried really worked and he could get through a night without assistance. Once you've done it a couple times, strike off on solo overnight trips to hone your skills. The freedom you feel will be immense and your confidence will be solidified.

Chapter 14 – Additional Reading

This book has been a broad, basic introduction on how to stay alive in the wilderness and return home safely. The following books present more comprehensive examinations of particular subject areas.

- *Wilderness 911* by Eric Weiss

- *Compass & Map Navigator* by Michael Hodgson

- *Basic Essentials: Using GPS* by Bruce Grubbs (Falcon Guide)

- *Desert Survival* by Tony Nester

- *Northern Bushcraft* by Mors Kochanski

- *Primitive Wilderness Living & Survival Skills* by John and Geri McPherson

- *Outdoor Survival Skills* by Larry Olsen

- *Tom Brown's Field Guide to Wilderness Survival* by Tom Brown

- *Field Guide to North American Edible Wild Plants* by S. Elias and A. Dykeman

Chapter 15 – Equipment and Information Resources

Survival Kits

www.adventuremedicalkits.com

www.coughlans.com

www.mpioutdoors.com

www.tmru.org (Tacoma Mountain Rescue Unit)

www.northstarsurvival.com

www.prosurvivalkit.com

Clothing

www.rangerjoes.com

www.cabelas.com

www.woolcamo.com

www.dayonecamouflage.com

www.golite.com

Maps

www.topo.com

www.nationalgeographic.com/topo

www.usfs.gov (U.S. Forest Service)

www.blm.gov (U.S. Bureau of Land Management)

www.doi.gov (U.S Department of the Interior)

www.maps.yahoo.com

Compasses

www.marblesoutdoors.com

www.silvacompass.com

www.rangerjoes.com

GPS

www.garmin.com

Shelter

www.adventuremedicalkits.com

www.rangerjoes.com

www.cabelas.com

www.golite.com

www.kifaru.net

www.hennessyhammock.com

Fire

www.ultimatesurvival.com

www.lightmyfireusa.com

www.brunton.com

Water

www.steripen.com

www.msrgear.com

www.katadyn.com

www.mcnett.com

Signal

www.rangerjoe.com

www.orionsignals.com

www.cellsafe.com

First Aid

www.adventuremedicalkits.com

www.redcross.org

www.nols.edu/wmi

www.wildmed.com

www.wildernessmedicine.com

Challenging Conditions

www.nws.noaa.gov; (National Weather Service)

www.oregoninstruments.com

www.weather.com

Chapter 16 – Survival Kits

For a small, basic kit (this is my personal kit):

- Sharp, sturdy knife with saw blade

- Emergency "sleeping bag" made of strong material

- Fifty feet of 1/8" nylon cord

- Micro-headlamp (LED)

- Strike-anywhere matches in waterproof container

- Storm-proof lighter

- Metal match

- One dozen cotton balls saturated with petroleum jelly, stored in a 35mm film canister

- Three WetFire tinder cubes

- Frontier water filter straw

- Marble's button compass

- Signal mirror

- Whistle

- One-gallon re-sealable plastic bag

- Four water purification tablets

- Fishing kit

- Snare wire

For bigger kits (all items above, plus):

- Hatchet

- Food rations

- Metal cup

- Shelter piece (tarp, plastic, or poncho)

- Heavy-duty aluminum foil (folded into small square)

- 18" of hollow rubber tubing

- Communication device (cell phone, radio, etc)

- Water purification system (pump, bottle, or UV)

Other items to substitute or consider:

- Larger headlamp and extra batteries

- Parachute cord

- Base plate compass

- Personal Locator Beacon

- Emergency radio transmitter or satellite phone

Acknowledgements

Several of the chapters (and pieces of others) in this book appeared in shorter form as installments of the *Bowhunter Magazine Survival Series*, which has been running since October 2003. Thank you to Publisher Jeff Waring for permission to reprint the material. Special thanks to Editor Dwight Schuh and Assistant Editor Brian Fortenbaugh at *Bowhunter Magazine* for their support, mentorship, and guidance.

Thanks to Carl Weil, Gates Richards, and James Newberry for their expertise and willingness to answer questions.

My sister Heather Solomon is an outstanding photographer and took several of the pictures I used in this book. You can see more of her work at www.hasarts.com.

Thanks to Louise Nelson for editing some of the chapters.

Travis Horton modeled for several of the pictures in this book and we've spent many days in the woods together. I hope we have many more.

Jennifer and Ross Morgan, as well as the New Mexico Department of Game and Fish Hunter Education Program, deserve special recognition for their encouragement and support of survival workshops as part of Instructor development.

Lastly, thank you to my wonderful family, Ashley, Adam, and Sean, for their love and support.

About the Author

John Solomon is a freelance outdoor writer and former U.S. Air Force Survival Instructor. He is a masthead Contributor for *Bowhunter Magazine* and writes their regular Survival column. He also teaches Hunter Education and survival workshops for the New Mexico Department of Game and Fish. In addition to *Bowhunter*, his writing has appeared in *Petersen's Hunting, Rocky Mountain Game & Fish, Bugle, Fur-Fish-Game, Traditional Bowhunter,* and *Backwoodsman Magazine.* John is a Life Member of the International Hunter Education Association, a Sustaining Member of the Rocky Mountain Elk Foundation, and an Associate Member of the Pope & Young Club. He resides in Albuquerque, New Mexico.

Order this book online at www.trafford.com
or email orders@trafford.com

Most Trafford titles are also available at major online book retailers.

Printed in Victoria, BC, Canada.

ISBN: 978-1-4269-3025-6 (sc)

ISBN: 978-1-4269-3026-3 (e-book)

*Our mission is to efficiently provide the world's finest, most comprehensive book publishing
service, enabling every author to experience success. To find out how to publish your book, your
way, and have it available worldwide, visit us online at www.trafford.com*

Trafford rev. 3/23/2010

 www.trafford.com

North America & international
toll-free: 1 888 232 4444 (USA & Canada)
phone: 250 383 6864 ♦ fax: 812 355 4082